The Telegraph
Tax Guide 2022

The Telegraph
Tax Guide 2022

Jon Yarker

KoganPage

First published as *The Daily Telegraph Guide to Income Tax* in 1974 by Constable & Robinson Ltd
This edition published in Great Britain and the United States in 2022 by Kogan Page Limited

2nd Floor, 45 Gee Street	8 W 38th Street, Suite 902	4737/23 Ansari Road
London	New York, NY 10018	Daryaganj
EC1V 3RS	USA	New Delhi 110002
United Kingdom		India

www.koganpage.com

Kogan Page books are printed on paper from sustainable forests.

ISBNs

Hardback	978 1 3986 0835 1
Paperback	978 1 3986 0831 3
Ebook	978 1 3986 0834 4
ISSN	2514-3727

British Library Cataloguing-in-Publication Data

A CIP record for this book is available from the British Library.

Typeset by Integra Software Services, Pondicherry
Print production managed by Jellyfish
Printed and bound by CPI Group (UK) Ltd, Croydon CR0 4YY

CONTENTS

Appendices 265

ABOUT THE AUTHOR

Jon Yarker is a financial journalist and part of Rhotic Media, where he heads up the agency's features team. He has written for a wide range of leading financial services trade titles such as *Investment Week, Money Marketing, COVER, Professional Adviser, FT Adviser* and *Pensions Expert*.

Prior to joining Rhotic, a multi-award-winning agency offering editorial services and corporate content to a broad range of clients, he was a freelance writer. In addition to working as a marketing executive at a leading wealth management firm, he spent several years working full time as an investment correspondent for trade publications *Money Marketing* and *Citywire Wealth Manager*. He has written extensively on all areas of financial services, including tax, investment, regulation, insurance and advice, and carries the IMC qualification.

Introduction

We all want a better education for our children, an improved National Health Service, a more efficient and reliable transport system, less congestion on the roads and to feel safer and more secure in our homes and when we walk the streets. So who has to foot the bill for all these services? The government, of course. And how does the government raise the revenues to meet this expenditure? Mainly by taxing income, wealth, production and imports as well as collecting social contributions from us. Any deficit from one year to the next is funded by borrowing.

Several taxes and benefits are covered in this guide:

- Income Tax – what we pay annually on our earnings, pensions and income from savings.
- Capital Gains Tax – only paid when we realize profits on sales of some types of asset.
- Inheritance Tax – chargeable on some lifetime gifts of capital and on the value of our estates on death.
- Value Added Tax – included in the price of many goods and services we buy.
- National Insurance – the contributions we have to pay based on our earnings or business profits.
- Social Security – various benefits, including the State Pension, we may be able to claim.
- Tax credits – whether you are eligible and how to work out what you can claim.

For many people tax is both confusing and complicated. This book aims to:

- explain the basics of the taxes covered for the average taxpayer as straightforwardly as possible;
- help readers have a better understanding of their tax affairs and, therefore, be able to take control;
- make staying within the law as easy as possible; and
- help cut tax bills with pointers to saving on tax.

This edition of *The Telegraph Tax Guide* is primarily intended to cover the Self Assessment tax year from 6 April 2021 to 5 April 2022 and is being published soon after you need to submit a Tax Return for this year.

The tax changes announced by the Chancellor of the Exchequer in his 2021 Spring and Autumn Budgets are set out in the final chapter of the book.

I hope you benefit from the read.

Note that the HMRC forms in this book have been made as accurate as possible at the time of writing. Please visit GOV.UK for the most recent available HMRC forms.

01
You and HMRC

Ask any taxpayer the question 'Would you like to pay less tax?' and I imagine that, almost without exception, the answer would be 'Yes'. By the time you have finished reading this book I would like to think that you will have come across at least one way of saving tax. Maybe:

- another allowance or relief you can claim;
- an expense that could be included in your business accounts; or
- a more tax-efficient structuring of your cash savings and investments.

But, first of all, you should have an understanding of the workings of the various HM Revenue & Customs (HMRC) departments responsible for the day-to-day running of our tax system.

The board of HMRC has overall authority for administering the fiscal legislation enacted by government. Although there are a large number of specialist departments within HMRC, it is likely that your only contact with it will be through the staff at your tax office and the accounts offices.

Tax offices

Each tax office throughout the country is headed up by a senior officer with a full support staff. The tax affairs of employees and pensioners are looked after by the tax office that deals with the Pay As You Earn (PAYE) affairs of their employer or pension fund. If you are self-employed you may find that the tax office responsible for your tax affairs is sometimes local to your business address.

It is your service office that:

- sends you an email or letter telling you to complete a Tax Return;
- processes your Return when you send it back online or by post;
- corrects any obvious or simple errors that you have made and sends you a notice detailing the amendments; and
- initially chases you up if you are late submitting your Return.

Service offices are also responsible for:

- looking after all the day-to-day tax matters of the vast majority of taxpayers whose income is taxed under PAYE and do not come within the system of Self Assessment; and

- processing the business accounts of self-employed taxpayers.

As long as you comply with all your tax obligations in a timely manner, your only involvement with HMRC will be confined to your service office.

Wealthy taxpayers

If you are one of the wealthiest taxpayers, your tax affairs are looked after by one of the HMRC High Net Worth Units (HNWU). It is intended that each HNWU will:

- build relationships to help better understand these taxpayers and make it easier for them to get things right; and

- better tailor service delivery for these taxpayers through proactive engagement and by providing a single point of contact as well as a holistic approach for their tax affairs.

Taxpayers with particular needs

HMRC offer a range of facilities for taxpayers with particular needs; for example, if:

- you are blind or partially sighted;

- you are deaf, have impaired hearing or have a speech impediment; or

- your first language is not English.

If you think you need extra help, the number to call is 0300 200 3300. Those calling from outside the UK should call +(44) 135 535 9022.

Accounts offices

The main tasks of HMRC accounts offices are to:

- bank payments of tax and National Insurance Contributions; and

- keep up-to-date, accurate payments records.

If you need to telephone, write to or visit any of these offices, always give your name and reference number. You can find the address and telephone number on forms and letters that have been sent to you.

Dealing with HMRC

Information about the following is available to you by telephoning 0300 200 3300:

- personal information such as changes of address or in your personal circumstances;
- employment details;
- claims to personal allowances;
- claims to tax relief on either the flat-rate expenses listed in Appendix 1 or certain professional subscriptions by inclusion in your PAYE coding for the current year;
- employee benefits such as a company car, fuel for private motoring and medical insurance that affect your PAYE coding;
- notification of Gift Aid payments or contributions into your pension plan;
- savings and investment income;
- State and other pensions;
- taxable State benefits;
- income from renting out your home when you are away from it;
- income from letting out a room in your home;
- other property income;
- making certain amendments to your Self Assessment Return; and
- dealing with tax repayments due to you.

In most cases nothing more will be needed from you, although the call may lead to further action by HMRC (for example, sending out a revised PAYE Coding Notice). Where your business cannot be completely dealt with by telephone, the HMRC officer will arrange to send you any necessary forms or follow-up material.

When you telephone, do not be discouraged by any steps taken to establish your identity. Any such checks are for the purpose of safeguarding the privacy of your tax affairs.

On any matter that does not come within the 'business by telephone' services, I recommend you put any questions in writing to HMRC at: Pay as You Earn and Self Assessment, HM Revenue & Customs, BX9 1AS.

Whenever you telephone or write, always remember to quote your reference number, which is:

- your employer's PAYE reference; or
- your National Insurance number; or
- if you are self-employed or pay tax at the higher rate, your Self Assessment Unique Taxpayer Reference (UTR). This is a 10-digit number.

Personal tax account

By setting up a personal tax account, you can:

- check your records; and
- manage your tax affairs with HMRC.

It enables you to handle your tax affairs:

- online;
- promptly and simply; and
- whenever you choose to do so.

Furthermore, it is:

- secure;
- personalized; and
- assembles all your tax particulars in one place.

To sign in you will need:

- a Government Gateway account, which you will have if you have already used HMRC online services; and
- your National Insurance number.

Once you have signed in you can use your personal tax account for a range of services, for example to:

- complete, send and view your annual Tax Return;
- check your Income Tax estimate and tax code;

- claim a tax repayment;
- check or update your employment benefits, such as a company car or private medical insurance;
- review or update entitlement to the marriage allowance;
- tell HMRC when you move home;
- find your National Insurance number;
- check and manage any tax credits that you receive; and
- find out about your State Pension.

This is just a snapshot of what you can do. HMRC intend that more services will be added at a later date.

Compliance checks and enquiries

Once your Return has been processed by your tax office, it will undergo a comprehensive programme of checks. Any obvious errors, for example in your arithmetic, will be corrected. Alternatively, HMRC will write or telephone to resolve any queries relating to:

- your Self Assessment Tax Return;
- your accounts and tax calculations; and
- the taxes you pay.

In most cases, no further questions will be asked. But enquiries will be started by your tax office if:

- something requires fuller explanation;
- there is a risk your Return may be incorrect; or
- your Return is selected for enquiry at random.

Normally, HMRC have 12 months from the date that your Return is received by your tax office in which to tell you that it will be the subject of enquiries.

Your Return will normally become final if your tax office has not raised any enquiries within the permitted time period. HMRC can only raise enquiries at a later date if they discover an error that they could not reasonably have been expected to be aware of from the information provided in, or with, your Return.

At the end of an enquiry into your Return, HMRC will issue a closure notice, which will include the making of any necessary adjustments to your Self Assessment. You have 30 days in which to appeal against such amendments.

Any enquiries by your tax office should be conducted in accordance with the specific code of practice laid down by HMRC. If your Tax Return ever becomes the subject of an enquiry, this may well be a time when you should be represented by a professional tax adviser.

Determinations

Not surprisingly, HMRC has special powers to deal with taxpayers who are sent a Return but fail to complete it and submit it by the filing date. In such cases an offending taxpayer can expect HMRC to make a determination of his or her income and capital gains chargeable to tax to the best of their knowledge and belief. The actual amount of tax is based on estimates of:

- the taxpayer's allowances and reliefs; and
- tax deducted at source on earnings and savings income.

Any determination can be subsequently superseded by:

- a Self Assessment by the taxpayer; or
- HMRC based on information provided by the taxpayer.

Assessments and appeals

In cases of fraud or neglect, your Tax Inspector can raise an assessment to collect tax that should have been paid on a Self Assessment. You do, of course, have a right of appeal against:

- an assessment raised by your Tax Inspector; or
- an amendment to your Return following an enquiry.

The procedure for resolving your appeal starts with a hearing before an independent tribunal of expert tax judges and/or panel members. It can then move on to the courts and ultimately to the House of Lords.

Prosecutions

An important role of HMRC is to deter fraud. They will prosecute in serious cases in all areas of the tax system. Cases selected for prosecution involve a wide range of offences. However, a case is more likely to be considered for prosecution if it contains features such as:

- falsification of documents;
- lying during an investigation;
- conspiracy; or
- discovery of false documents made during an earlier investigation.

Your Charter

HMRC want to provide a service that is:

- fair;
- accurate; and
- based on mutual trust and respect.

HMRC are also committed to making it as easy as they can to get matters right. 'Your Charter' explains:

- what you can expect from HMRC; and
- what HMRC expect from you.

Your rights – what you can expect from HMRC

Respect you and treat you as honest

HMRC will:

- treat you even-handedly, with courtesy and respect;
- listen to your concerns and answer your questions clearly; and

- presume that you are telling the truth, unless they have good reason to think otherwise.

Provide a helpful, efficient and effective service
HMRC will:

- help you understand what you have to do and when you have to do it;
- deal with the information you give them quickly, efficiently, and keep any costs to a minimum; and
- put any mistakes right as soon as they can.

Be professional and act with integrity
HMRC will:

- act within the law and make sure you are dealt with by people who have the right level of expertise;
- help you understand your rights; and
- be sensitive to any financial difficulties you have.

Protect your information and respect your privacy
HMRC will:

- protect information they obtain, receive or hold about you;
- only share information about you when the law lets them; and
- explain why they need any additional information.

Accept that someone else can represent you
HMRC will:

- respect your wish to have someone else deal with them on your behalf, such as an accountant or relative;
- only deal with them if they have been authorized to represent you; and
- deal with them courteously and professionally.

Deal with complaints quickly and fairly
HMRC will:

- deal with your complaint or appeals as quickly as they can;
- let you ask someone else to look into an issue on your behalf; and

- allow you to ask someone who has not been involved in the dispute to work with them if you cannot resolve matters with them.

Tackle those who bend or break the rules

HMRC will:

- identify those who are not paying what they owe or are claiming more than they should and recover the money; and
- charge interest and penalties where appropriate and be reasonable in how they use their powers.

Your obligations – what HMRC expect from you

Be honest and respect their staff

HMRC expect you to:

- be truthful and act within the law;
- give them all the relevant facts and information about your taxes, entitlements, and any additional information they ask you for; and
- treat their staff with the respect that you expect from them.

Work with them to get things right

HMRC expect you to:

- work with them to make sure that your tax and payment affairs are right and that you are paying and claiming the correct amount of money; and
- talk to them if there is anything you are not sure about.

Find out what you need to do and keep them informed

HMRC expect you to:

- make sure you know how to pay your tax and claim payments;
- get in touch with them as soon as possible if you need help; and
- tell them straight away if you are having trouble meeting your obligations.

Keep accurate records and protect your information

HMRC expect you to:

- make sure that you, or your representative, keep accurate financial records that support what you tell them;

- not share confidential information with others; and
- tell them straight away if you think someone else knows your identification details, such as passwords.

Know what your representative does on your behalf

HMRC expect you to:

- know what information and payments your representative sends them; and
- make sure that the information and payments are accurate and on time.

Respond in good time

HMRC expect you to:

- send them Returns and pay any amounts you owe on time; and
- pay any interest on late payments or penalties promptly.

Take reasonable care to avoid mistakes

HMRC expect you to take care to avoid mistakes when you send them information, pay your taxes and claim any payments or reliefs.

Complaints

Any complaint should, first of all, be made to the tax office with which you are dealing, either by telephone, in writing or online. Address your letter to the Officer in Charge:

- describe the complaint (for example, slow service, constant mistakes);
- what went wrong;
- when it happened;
- who dealt with you;
- what effect HMRC's actions had on you; and
- how you would like HMRC to resolve the problem.

Most complaints about HMRC's handling of people's tax affairs are satisfactorily settled by their tax office. Where taxpayers are not satisfied with the response from their office, they can take their case to a different complaints handler.

Taxpayers who are still dissatisfied can put their case to the HMRC Adjudicator, who will review all the facts and try to reach a decision as soon as possible. HMRC normally accept this decision unless there are exceptional circumstances.

Taxpayers can also ask a Member of Parliament to refer their complaint to the Parliamentary and Health Service Ombudsman. The Ombudsman, who is independent, will look into a complaint, but usually after it has first of all been considered by the Adjudicator.

Changes in legislation

The Chancellor of the Exchequer makes an annual Budget Statement. Between 2016 and 2018 the Budget was in the autumn, but in 2019 the Budget was moved from the autumn to spring 2020. Not only does he – and since 1221 every holder of the post has been a man – use this occasion to report on the nation's finances, but he also tells us about:

- tax rates and allowances for the following year; and
- new or amending legislation to our tax laws.

Resulting legislative changes are published in a Finance Bill. Its various clauses are debated by Parliament and occasionally amended. Subsequently, the Bill is passed by both Houses of Parliament before receiving Royal Assent. It is then published as a Finance Act.

When the law is either unclear or ambiguous, HMRC will issue a Statement of Practice indicating how they intend to interpret it. There are also times when HMRC do not seek to go by the strict letter of the law. These are gathered together and published as a list of Extra-Statutory Concessions.

02
Tax rates and allowances

For most of us our annual tax bill is determined by:

- tax bands and rates; and
- the allowances we can claim.

Income Tax rates

Under our tax system, the tax (or fiscal) year runs from each 6 April to the following 5 April. The rates of tax for 2021/2022 are:

Band of taxable income (£)	Rate of tax (%)	Tax on band (£)	Cumulative tax (£)
0–37,700	20	7,540	7,540
37,701–150,000	40	44,920	52,460
Over 150,000	45		

The rates of 20 per cent and 40 per cent are respectively known as the basic and higher rates. The additional rate refers to tax at the 45 per cent level.

There are special rules and rates for working out the tax you pay on your savings and dividend incomes (see Chapter 10).

Scottish Income Tax rates

You will pay Scottish Income Tax if:

- your main home is in Scotland; or
- you move to Scotland and live there for more than half the tax year.

The rates of tax for 2021/22 are:

Band of taxable income (£)	Rate of tax (%)	Tax on band (£)	Cumulative tax (£)
0–2,097	19	398.43	398.43
2,098 to 12,726	20	2,125.80	2,524.23
12,727 to 31,092	21	3,856.86	5,982.66
31,093–150,000	41	48,752.28	52,609.14
Over 150,000	46		

Scottish Income Tax is payable on:

- your wages, pension; and
- most other taxable income.

But you pay the same tax as the rest of the UK on your savings income and dividends.

Allowances

The rates of the various tax allowances for 2021/22 are:

	£
Personal	
All individuals	12,570*
Married couples	
Either spouse/partner born before 6 April 1935	9,125**/***
Minimum amount	3,530***
Marriage	
Transferable marriage allowance	1,260 ****
Relief for blind person (each)	2,520

* The personal allowance reduces at the rate of £1 for every £2 of income in excess of £100,000.

** The married couple's allowance comes down by £1 for every £2 of income above a specified limit – £30,400 for 2021/22.

*** Indicates allowances where tax relief is restricted to 10 per cent.

**** Available to spouses/civil partners born after 5 April 1935.

In working out the amount of Income Tax payable each year:

- the personal, blind person's and transferred marriage allowances are taken off total income; and
- tax relief for the married couple's allowance is given as a deduction from tax payable.

Personal allowance

Every man, woman or child, single or married and resident in the United Kingdom can claim the personal allowance. This is set against total taxable income from all sources, such as:

- a wage, salary or business profits;
- an occupational and/or a State Pension;
- interest on savings;
- income from investments; and
- rental income.

During 2021/22, Richard West, a married man in his early 40s, earned £36,500 from his job. His tax liability for the year is £4,786, worked out as follows:

	£
Salary	36,500
Less: Personal allowance	12,570
Taxable income	23,930
Income Tax payable	
£24,000 @ 20 per cent	4,786

Paul Frost received remuneration, including benefits, of £110,000 during 2021/22. His tax liability for the year amounted to £33,432, worked out as follows:

	£
Remuneration	110,000
Less: Personal allowance	7,570
Taxable income	102,430

	£
Income Tax payable	
£37,700 @ 20 per cent	7,540
£64,730 @ 40 per cent	25,892
	33,432

Your Personal Allowance goes down by £1 for every £2 that your adjusted net income is above £100,000. Therefore, Paul's personal allowance for the year is reduced by £5,000 being 1/2 x (£110,000 – £100,000) from £12,570 to £7,570.

Tax Saver

The marginal rate of tax on income in the band from £100,000 to £125,000 is 40 per cent. If your net income is somewhere in this band the payment of:

- Gift Aid donations (see Chapter 4); and/or
- allowable pension contributions (see Chapter 9),

is very tax efficient.

Marriage allowance

You can claim the marriage allowance if all of the following requirements apply:

- you are married or in a civil partnership;
- both of you were born on or after 6 April 1935;

- your income for 2021/22 is not more than £12,570, plus up to £5,000* of savings income; and

- your spouse or partner's income for 2021/22 is between £12,571 and £50,270.

*After taking off your Personal Savings Allowance.

Tax Saver

The marriage allowance enables you to transfer £1,260 of your 2021/22 personal allowance to your spouse or partner. By so doing you will save tax of £252 (£1,260 @20 per cent).

Clearly it is only advantageous to claim the marriage allowance in cases where one spouse or civil partner is unable to claim all or part of their personal allowance because of a low income.

You can apply for the marriage allowance by registering online at www.gov.uk/apply-marriage-allowance. If your application is accepted, the changes to your own and your spouse's/partner's personal allowances will be backdated to the beginning of the tax year.

If you or your spouse/partner were born before 6 April 1935 you may be able to claim the married couple's allowance (see below).

Other features of this measure are:

- the allowance is transferable in full or not at all; and

- it will always be equivalent to 10 per cent of the rounded-up personal allowance.

Married couple's allowance

You can claim the married couple's allowance if you can satisfy all of the following:

- you are married or in a civil partnership;

- one of you was born before 6 April 1935; and

- you are living together.

It is the husband's income which is used to calculate the married couple's allowance for a couple married before 5 December 2005. For marriage and civil partnerships after this date it is the person with the higher income.

Tax Saver

For 2021/22 the married couple's allowance could lower your tax bill from anywhere between £353 and £912.50 a year.

Tax Saver

For some reason you may not be able to live with your spouse or civil partner. This may be because:

- a spouse or partner needs to be in residential care owing to illness or old age;
- your job takes you away from home;
- you are in education or training; or
- you are in prison.

When you are living apart through any of these circumstances you can still claim the married couple's allowance.

Eric Black was 86 years old in 2021/22. His younger wife, Myra, celebrated her 68th birthday the same year. They are entitled to allowances of £21,695 and £12,570 as follows:

	Eric (£)	Myra (£)
Personal allowance	12,570	12,570
Married couple's allowance	9,125	
Total allowances	21,695	12,570

Long-standing partners Rex Gardner and Gerald Sullivan entered into a civil partnership on 4 January 2016. They are both in their late-80s. Gerald, who has the higher income, can claim the married couple's allowance of £9,125 for 2021/22.

The amount of the married couple's allowance in the year of marriage:

- depends upon the time in the year that the wedding takes place; and
- is reduced by one-twelfth for every complete month from 6 April up to the day of the marriage.

Percy Hughes, aged 87, married his wife, Barbara, aged 73, on 10 November 2021. He receives an allowance of £3,802 for 2021/22, worked out as follows:

	£
Married couple's allowance	9,125
Less: Reduction	
7/12 × £9,125	5,323
2021/22 allowance	3,802

There is no reduction in the married couple's allowance for a year when:

- couples separate;
- couples divorce; or
- one spouse dies (a widow is entitled to any unused part of the married couple's allowance for the year in which she loses her husband).

Tax Saver

If you cannot benefit from the full amount of the married couple's allowance because:

- you are not a taxpayer; or
- your tax bill is not big enough,

you can transfer the balance to your spouse or partner by completing form 575(T).

A wife does not need her husband's consent to claim one half of the minimum amount of the married couple's allowance, £1,765 for 2021/22. Alternatively, a married couple can jointly elect for the wife to receive the full minimum amount of the allowance, £3,530 for 2021/22. Such an election:

- must be made using HMRC Form 18;

- must normally be made before the start of the tax year for which it is to apply (except in the year of marriage, when the newly-weds can submit a notice dealing with the reduced married couple's allowance for that year); and
- once made carries on from year to year until changed by the couple.

James Lucas, who is in his late-80s, had income from pensions of £14,000 in 2021/22. His wife, Mary, who is 20 years younger than James, is still working and earned a salary of £15,500 in 2021/22. She elected to receive one half of the basic married couple's allowance. James does not pay any tax for 2021/22 as follows:

	£
Pensions	14,000
Less: Personal allowance	12,570
Taxable income	1,430
Income Tax payable	
£1,430 @ 20 per cent	286
Less: Relief for married couple's allowance	736
£9,125 – (1/2 × £3,530) = £7,360 @ 10 per cent	

Mary has a tax bill for the year of £409.50 as follows:

	£
Salary	15,500
Less: Personal allowance	12,570
Taxable income	2,930
Income Tax payable	
2,930 @ 20 per cent	586
Less: Relief for married couple's allowance	176.50
£1,765 (1/2 × £3,530) @ 10 per cent	
	409.50

The unused part of James's married couple's allowance amounts to £1,765. By making a claim, this can be transferred to Mary, thereby reducing her tax bill by 353 (£3,530 @ 10 per cent) from £409.50 to £56.

The purpose of the married couple's allowance is to assist elderly taxpayers on low and modest incomes. It follows, therefore, that this allowance is restricted when total income, after permitted reliefs and deductions, exceeds a specified limit – £30,400 in 2021/22. The reduction is £1 for each £2 by which total income is more than the annual stated limit.

However, there is a minimum amount of £3,530 for the married couple's allowance.

The upper income limit beyond which the married couple's allowance reduces to the minimum amount for £30,400 is 2021/22.

Blind person's relief

This relief is given to a registered blind person. Where both husband or wife or civil partners are:

- blind; or
- have severely impaired sight,

each of them can claim the relief. If either of them is on a low income and unable to use up his or her relief, any unused part can be transferred to the other even if he or she is not blind.

When a taxpayer first becomes entitled to this special relief, by being registered blind, the relief will also be given for the previous tax year if, at the time, the individual had received the necessary proof of blindness needed to qualify for registration. This concession prevents individuals losing out as a result of any delays in the registration process.

The relief is not available to registered partially sighted individuals.

03
Tax credits

Tax Saver

If you are on a low or modest income you should be able to claim tax credits. These are:

- Child Tax Credit (CTC), which is paid to individuals who are responsible for children. It does not matter whether claimants do, or do not, work.
- Working Tax Credit (WTC), which is paid to those in work and is targeted at low wage earners and workers who use formal childcare.

Who can claim?

To qualify for tax credits you must be:

- at least 16 years old; and
- physically present in the United Kingdom.

A single joint application must be submitted by:

- married couples;
- couples living together as partners; or
- civil partners.

Both tax credits are dependent on the incomes of the claimants.

You cannot make a new claim for tax credits if you live in an area of the country where Universal Credit (see Chapter 8) has been introduced.

Child Tax Credit

CTC is:

- available to individuals responsible for at least one child or qualifying young person; and
- paid by direct transfer to the bank account of the person (usually the mother) mainly responsible for the care of the child or children.

A child is a person under 16 years old or, in the case of a 16-year-old teenager, until 31 August after their 16th birthday.

A qualifying young person is someone who is:

- no longer a child;
- under 20 years old; and
- in full-time education, usually at a school or college; or
- on an approved training course.

You are usually responsible for a child if:

- they live with you permanently;
- you are their main carer and they normally live with you;
- their toys and clothes are kept in your home; or
- you feed them and give them spending money.

If you share responsibility for a child and you cannot reach agreement on which of you claims, you can both apply. In this situation the Tax Credit Office will make the decision.

CTC is made up of the following elements:

Rates for 2021/22	Annual (£)	Weekly (£)
Family element	545.00	10.48
Child element (each child)	2,830.00	54.42
Disabled child element*	3,435.00	66.06
Severely disabled child element**	1,390.00	26.73

*In addition to the child element.
**As well as the child and disabled child elements.

What you will get depends on:

- whether you are already receiving CTC; and
- the date when your claim started.

Elements of CTC	Date claim started	
	Before 6 April 2017	On or after 6 April 2017
Family element	Yes	Only if one child was born before 6 April 2017
Child element	All children born before 6 April 2017*	Up to 2 children only

* You will only get the child element for a baby born after 6 April 2017 if the baby is your second child.

Working Tax Credit

To qualify for WTC you must be:

- between 16 and 24 years old, have a child or be disabled; or
- aged 25 or over, with or without children.

You have to work a specific number of hours in a week to receive WTC as follows:

Your situation	Working hours per week
Age 25–59	30 hours minimum
Over 60 years old	16 hours minimum
Disabled	16 hours minimum
Single with at least one child	16 hours minimum
Couple with one or more children	Normally at least 24 hours between them – one has to work for at least 16 hours

There are special rules for some couples:

- with at least one child; and
- who work for less than 24 hours a week between them.

You can claim if you work a minimum of 16 hours a week and:

- you are disabled;
- at least 60 years old; or
- your partner is entitled to Carer's Allowance or is in hospital or prison.

Your work can be:

- for someone else as a worker or as an employee;
- for yourself as a self employed person; or
- as a combination of the two.

If you are self-employed:

- you must be in business to make a profit; and
- your work has to be on a proper commercial footing.

Recipients of WTC may also qualify for assistance with the costs of child-care. To be entitled you must be:

- a lone working parent;
- a couple, both of whom work, with one or both responsible for a child or children; or
- a couple, one of whom works and the other is either incapacitated, a hospital in-patient or in prison.

The childcare element of WTC is paid, with entitlement to WTC, to the person responsible for the care of the child or children. WTC comprises the following elements:

Rates for 2021/22	Annual (£)	Weekly (£)
Basic entitlement	2,005	38.55
Additional couples, and lone parent, element	2,060	39.32
30-hour element	830	15.96
Disability element	3,240	62.30
Severe disability element	1,400	26.92
Childcare element		
• maximum eligible cost		300.00
• maximum eligible cost for one child		175.00
Percentage of eligible cost covered		70%

Income limits

As an indication, you are probably entitled to tax credits if your annual income is below the following.

For CTC, without childcare costs:

- £25,000 – if you have one child;
- £35,000 – if you have two children.

For WTC:

- £13,100 – if you are single with no children; and
- £18,000 – if you are married or in a couple without children.

How to claim

To make your first claim you will need to complete form TC600. You can do so by either:

- using the 'Find out if you qualify for tax credits' online facility; or
- calling the Tax Credits Office on 0345 300 3900.

When you telephone, you will be asked for:

- your National Insurance number (see Chapter 8);
- your income for the previous tax year;
- details of any childcare payments;
- information about any benefits you receive; and
- the number of hours you work each week.

If you are told that you are entitled to tax credits you should also:

- be given an estimate of how much you will receive; and
- be sent a claim form which can take up to two weeks to reach you.

The completed form should either be:

- returned to the address on the form; or
- handed in to your Jobcentre Plus if you are on benefits.

Tax Saver

Do not delay in making your claim since it can only be backdated for a maximum of 31 days.

Payment

HMRC pay both CTC and WTC to the main carer at either weekly or four-weekly intervals. Where there is a joint claim, the couple can jointly nominate the main carer. If they fail to do so:

- HMRC will make the decision; and
- nominate the main carer, who will usually be the mother or the person receiving Child Benefit.

Tax credits and other benefits

If you receive tax credits, you may get less:

- income-based Jobseeker's Allowance;
- Income Support;
- income-related Employment and Support Allowance;
- Housing Benefit; or
- State Pension Credit.

The office that deals with the payment of your benefits will be able to work out how these are affected by tax credits.

Tapering

Tax credits taper away at a rate of 41 per cent for each £1 of family income over a threshold of £6,565 (£16,480 where no WTC is claimed). The first £300 of income from pensions, savings and property is excluded. The order of reduction is:

- WTC;
- childcare element of WTC;
- child elements of CTC; and
- family element of CTC.

Tax Saver

For taxpayers claiming tax credits and paying pension contributions, not only will they see their tax bill come down but they may also qualify for an increase in their tax credits award as pension contributions reduce income for tax credit purposes.

Malcolm and Fiona Gifford are married and have three children, one of whom is disabled. Malcolm works full time, earning £26,200 in 2021/22. Fiona works part time and in the same year earned £7,800 for her 20-hour week.
   Their entitlement to tax credits for 2021/22 is £6,162 as follows:

	£	£
WTC		
Basic entitlement	2,005	
Additional couple's element	2,060	
30-hour element	830	
		4,895
CTC		
Child element (3)	8,535	
Disabled child element	3,435	
Family element	545	12,515
		17,410
Income	34,000	
Less: Threshold	6,565	
	27,435	
41 per cent thereof		11,248
Total Credits for 2021/22		6,162

Rachel Carson, who looks after her two young sons, is a successful businesswoman on a salary of £45,000 for 2021/22. As Rachel is a single parent she has to pay for childcare and this costs her £280 per week. Her tax credits for 2021/22 work out at £5,564 as follows:

	£	£
WTC		
Basic entitlement	2,005	
Lone parent element	2,060	
30-hour element	830	
Childcare element*	10,192	15,087
CTC		
Child element (2)	5,690	
Family element	545	6,235
		21,322
Less: Taper 41 per cent × £38,435 (£45,000 − £6,565)		15,758
Total Credits for 2021/22		5,564

*£196 per week being 70 per cent of the cost of £280 per week.

Annual renewal

Every year between April and June each existing claimant will receive a renewal pack that serves two purposes:

- first, to establish actual income for the year just ended and to check on the claimant's circumstances; and

- second, to make the claim for the new year.

You have until 31 July to complete and return the forms. Once the information you have provided has been processed, you will receive a notice about your final tax credit for the year recently ended.

If you have received too much tax credit you will be expected to refund the excess. This will usually be done by restricting the reward for the year following.

If you have been paid too little tax credit you will receive the extra amount as a single payment.

Changes in circumstances

Once a claimant has been granted tax credits, even for a nil amount, he or she has a duty to advise HMRC online, or by post or telephone, within 30 days of certain stipulated changes in circumstances, which are:

- marriage, moving in to live with a partner or entering a civil partnership;
- divorce, separation from, or death of, a partner;
- a child or partner dies;
- a child over 16 leaves either education, training or a careers service;
- a child moves out, goes into care or is taken into custody;
- a drop of more than £10 a week in the average costs of childcare;
- discontinuing payment to a childcare provider;
- childcare provider ceases to be registered or approved;
- working hours falling below 30 a week (16 if you are claiming childcare costs);
- working hours falling below, or going above, the minimum required to qualify;
- going abroad for at least eight weeks; and/or
- leaving the United Kingdom permanently.

You should also notify HMRC as soon as you can of other changes, which include:

- the birth of a child;
- change of address, bank details or childcare provider;
- you start paying for, or stop getting help with, the costs of approved childcare;
- you begin claiming benefits or any of your existing benefits change;
- a child is certified blind;
- someone in the household becomes disabled; or
- a change to your working hours from under 30 a week to 30 or more.

Income disregard

Not only is a claimant's entitlement to tax credits continuously adjusted by alterations in lifestyle circumstances but it is also affected by changes to income in the award period, namely a tax year.

When a claimant's income drops, a higher award can be immediately requested. However, a drop in income of up to £2,500 in a claim year is disregarded in assessing any increase in entitlement.

Conversely, when income increases the amount of the award will come down. However, a claimant's income for tax credit purposes can increase by as much as £2,500 in a claim year, compared to the previous year, without any reduction in entitlement. This gives more certainty to claimants that their payments will not suddenly be decreased when their income goes up during an award period.

Any change in annual income of £2,500 or more, up or down, must be reported immediately.

Penalties and interest

The following penalties can be charged:

Offence	Penalty
Failure to notify a change of in-year circumstances or to provide information or evidence required by HMRC	An initial penalty of £300 followed by penalties of up to £60 per day for continuing failure
Over claiming tax credits	Variable depending on mistake or misunderstanding, failure to take reasonable care, serious or deliberate error
Making negligent or fraudulent claims, statements or declarations	Up to £3,000

Interest may be charged by HMRC where tax credits are overpaid, wholly or partly, because of neglect or fraud by a claimant.

Help and advice

If you would like help or advice about tax credits, you can:

- phone the Helpline on 0345 300 3900 (England, Scotland and Wales) or 0345 603 2000 (Northern Ireland);
- go online to www.gov.uk/taxcredits; or
- visit a local advice service such as a Citizens Advice who may be able to help.

04

Interest payments and other outgoings

The opportunities for claiming tax relief on interest paid on borrowings are few and far between. They are for:

- the purchase, in certain circumstances, of life annuities if you are aged 65 or over;
- buying a share in:
  - an employee-controlled company;
  - a close company (ie controlled by five or fewer shareholders), or lending capital to it;
  - a partnership, or contributing capital to a partnership, if you are a partner; or
- buying plant and machinery for use in your job or partnership so long as the plant and machinery attracts capital allowances for tax purposes (see Chapter 7).

Interest is also allowable for tax purposes on a replacement loan where the interest on existing borrowings qualifies for tax relief.

It is important to understand that the purpose for which a loan is advanced governs whether the interest on it will be eligible for tax relief. How the loan is secured is not relevant.

Other than interest paid on a loan taken out to acquire buy-to-let property, the interest on which tax relief is due is deducted from your total income in the year of payment. It cannot be spread over the period of accrual, nor can tax relief be claimed if the interest is not actually paid.

> **Tax Saver**
>
> As you do not get tax relief on mortgage interest to buy your own home, it might be worthwhile using any spare cash on deposit with a bank or building society to repay some or all of your mortgage. This is particularly pertinent now, when interest rates on savings are so low.

Home annuity loans

Interest on a loan taken out before 9 March 1999 to purchase an annuity (an investment providing a fixed or increasing annual sum) from an insurance company still attracts tax relief at 23 per cent provided:

- the borrower was at least 65 years old at the time the annuity was purchased;
- not less than 90 per cent of the loan on which the interest is payable went towards buying an annuity for life; or
- security for the loan is the borrower's main residence.

The maximum loan on which tax relief is allowed is £30,000. Where a loan exceeds this limit, tax relief is given on the proportion of the total interest payable equivalent to the £30,000 limit. Income Tax at the special rate of 23 per cent will be deducted at source by the insurance company in working out the regular payments to be made by the borrower.

Buy-to-let: finance costs

Tax relief on finance costs such as interest on:

- mortgages;
- overdrafts; and
- loans, including those to purchase furnishings,

is restricted for individuals who receive rental income from letting residential property both in the UK and overseas.

From the 2020/21 tax year onwards, these individuals have been prohibited from deducting mortgage expenses from their rental income. Instead, they receive a tax credit based on 20 per cent of their mortgage interest payments.

In previous tax years the finance costs:

- fully deductible from rental income; and
- only attracting tax relief at the basic rate,

were as follows:

Tax year	Deducted from rental income (%)	Relief at the basic rate (%)
2017/18	75	25
2018/19	50	50
2019/20	25	75
2020/21	0	0

Ryan Morgan received a salary of £45,000 from his employer in 2021/22. His rental income, after allowable expenses, was £12,000 in the same year. He paid mortgage interest of £9,000 on loans taken out to acquire his let properties. His tax liability for the year is £9,552, calculated as follows:

	£	£
Salary		45,000
Net rental income	12,000	
Less: Tax credit (£9,000 × 20 per cent)	1,800	10,200
		55,200
Less: Personal Allowance		12,570
Taxable income		42,630
Income Tax payable		
£37,500 @ 20 per cent		7,500
£5,130 @ 40 per cent		2,052
		9,552

Any finance costs which:

- you have incurred in a tax year; and
- are not used to work out your tax reduction at the basic rate,

can be carried forward to the following year.

Business loans

Interest on any borrowings by your business can count as a deduction from your business profits for tax purposes. Provided that the borrowed money is issued for business purposes it does not matter whether the interest is paid on:

- a loan taken out for some specific purpose; or
- borrowings because your bank account goes overdrawn.

Interest you pay will also qualify for tax relief where you need to borrow to:

- buy an asset, such as a car or a piece of machinery, for use in your business (the tax allowable interest will be restricted by the extent of any private usage); or
- purchase a share in a partnership of which you are about to become a member, or contribute capital for use in its business.

Perhaps, however, you have business connections with a private company? Interest paid on a loan raised so you can either buy shares in the company, or lend it money for use in its business, is tax deductible. You must either:

- own at least 5 per cent of the company's share capital; or
- hold at least some shares in the company and spend the greater part of your time working in the business.

Employees who need to borrow to buy shares in their company, as part of an employee buy-out, are allowed tax relief on the interest paid on their borrowings.

Gift Aid

Tax Saver

Gift Aid is an Income Tax relief for cash gifts, without limit, by individuals to charities. Under Gift Aid a charity can claim back from HMRC 25p for every £1 you donate.

You can:

- give any amount, large or small, regularly or as a one-off donation; and
- pay by cash, cheque, postal order, standing order, direct debit, or by using your credit or debit card.

For your donation to qualify under Gift Aid you must:

- pay at least as much tax in the tax year in which you make your cash gifts as the charities will reclaim on them; and
- make a declaration to the charity, either orally or in writing, that you want your donation to be regarded as made under Gift Aid.

Tax Saver

If you pay tax at either the 40 per cent or 45 per cent rates, you can claim tax relief on your Gift Aid donations. This is worked out on the difference between the top rate at which you pay and the basic rate of 20 per cent.

Therefore, for every £100 you donate:

Your top rate of tax (%)	Your tax saving (£)	What the charity receives (£)
40	30.00	125.00
45	36.25	125.00

Norman Walton gave donations totalling £2,400 under Gift Aid in 2021/22. Norman is a higher rate taxpayer so he can reduce his tax bill by £600 as follows:

	£
Grossed-up donations – £2,400 × (100/80)	3,000
Tax relief thereon at 40 per cent	1,200
Less: Deducted when making donations	600
Reduction in Income Tax payable	600

Tax Saver

You can claim to carry back donations so they are treated as if paid in the previous tax year. For example, they can be carried back to 2020/21 so you get the tax relief in that year rather than in 2021/22, provided the donations were:

- made after 5 April 2021; and
- before 31 January 2022 – or the date when you send your 2020/21 Tax Return to your tax office (if earlier).

If you do not pay tax, Gift Aid is not for you.

Gifts of assets to charities

Tax Saver

You can claim relief from both Income Tax and Capital Gains Tax at your top rates of both taxes for the full market value of any gifts of shares, securities or land and buildings to charities at the time of the gift.

The assets that qualify for this type of tax relief are:

- shares or securities listed on a recognized Stock Exchange;
- shares or securities dealt in on any market in the United Kingdom that is designated for this purpose by HMRC;
- units in an authorized unit trust;
- shares in an open-ended investment company;
- an interest in an offshore fund; and
- land and buildings.

Jennifer Pickard pays tax at the higher rate of 40 per cent on a substantial part of her income. In September 2021 she decided to give shares in a quoted company valued at £8,000 to her favourite charity. The taxable capital gain on the shares would have been £3,600 if she had sold them. Jennifer saves tax of £3,920 as follows:

	£
Reduction in Income Tax (40 per cent × £8,000)	3,200
Capital Gains Tax not payable on the gain* (20 per cent × £3,600)	720
2021/22 Maximum tax saving	3,920

*Assuming Jennifer had already utilized her Annual Exemption Limit (see Chapter 13).

Payroll giving

If you are in employment there may be another way that you can make tax-efficient gifts to charity. But, first of all, you need to enquire if your employer participates in such an arrangement through a charity arrangement approved by HMRC. If so you can ask your employer to make regular deductions from your salary that, as part of the scheme, will be passed on to the charities of your choice. You will receive full Income Tax relief on such donations. There is no limit to the amount you can contribute this way each year.

Tax Saver

To give £100 costs:

- £80 if you pay tax at the basic rate;
- £60 for a higher rate taxpayer; and
- £55 for someone paying tax at the additional rate.

05
Working in employment

Most of us have worked for somebody else at some stage in our lives either on a full-time or part-time basis.

Am I employed?

Generally speaking you are regarded as employed:

- if you work for the same organization from day to day; and
- you do not have the risks associated with the running of a business.

If the answer is 'yes' to most of the following questions then you will correctly have been categorized as having employee status.

- Do you have to do the work yourself?
- Can you be told where to work, when to work, how to work and what to do?
- Can you be moved from job to job?
- Do you have to work a set number of hours?
- Are you paid a regular wage or salary?
- Can you get additional pay for overtime and a bonus?
- Are you entitled to holiday pay and sickness pay when you are away from work unwell?
- Are you responsible for managing anyone else engaged by your employer?

Earnings

The earnings from an employment on which Income Tax is payable are:

- a salary or wage;
- a bonus;
- overtime;
- commission;
- tips or gratuities;
- holiday or sick pay;
- part-time earnings;
- director's salary or fees; and
- benefits-in-kind.

The Pay As You Earn (PAYE) system

The mechanism for collecting the tax due on earnings from an employment is the PAYE system. It is the responsibility of employers to:

- deduct both Income Tax and National Insurance Contributions from the earnings of their employees; and
- pay the total deductions over to HMRC every month.

The PAYE deducted from an employee's earnings is regarded as a credit against the total tax payable by the employee for that tax year. Each employee's individual allowances and reliefs are taken into account by the employer in working out the amount of tax to deduct from the employee's salary or wage. This is possible because HMRC issue all employers with a code number for each employee.

Code numbers

Every employee's annual PAYE Coding Notice sets out:

- on the first lines, the total tax allowances due; and
- on the lines below, the amounts taken away from the allowances.

On the reverse of the form are guidance notes to help you understand how HMRC work out your tax code.

The PAYE system allows for the net allowances to be spread evenly throughout the tax year in working out the deductions for Income Tax so as to avoid any substantial variation to the amount of your regular salary cheque or pay packet.

All things being equal this system should ensure that the right amount of tax is deducted from your earnings each year. However, it can only work properly and effectively if you promptly tell your tax office of changes in your personal circumstances that affect any of the entries on your Notice of Coding. For example, most Coding Notices for the 2021/22 tax year, beginning on 6 April 2021, were sent out during the early part of the year. This is before your tax office will have received your 2020/21 Tax Return, stating your income, capital gains, reliefs and allowances for the year to 5 April 2021. It follows, therefore, that the information on which all 2021/22 code numbers have been based is out of date. This is why it is important that you check your code number for 2021/22 and tell your tax office if:

- alterations are required to your allowances of reliefs;
- you have changed jobs or ceased to be employed;
- you have started receiving a pension;
- there has been a big change in your income; or
- you have moved home.

Tax allowances for 2021/22 are:

	£
Personal	12,570
Transferable marriage	1,260
Married couples – maximum	9,125
Married couples – minimum	3,530
Blind persons	2,520

Figure 5.1 is an illustration of Simon Black's 2021/22 Notice of Coding. Simon is a married man, with two young children.

Figure 5.1 Notice of Coding

HM Revenue
& Customs

MR S BLACK
12 CHURCH RISE
BROADWOOD
PT3 8ZL

 35800

Dear MR S BLACK

National Insurance number   BZ 62 24 17 A

This is to tell you your tax code(s) for the year 6 April 2021 to 5 April 2022

Your tax code is used by your employer(s) and/or pension provider(s) to work out how much Income Tax to collect from your pay or pension. We send them a separate tax code notice.

This is how we worked out your tax code(s)

Your tax-free amount		For help
Personal Allowance	£12,570	Go to note 1
Total	£12,500	
Less Car Benefit	£4,400	Go to note 2
Less Car Fuel Benefit	£5,148	Go to note 3
Less Medical Insurance	£900	Go to note 4
Less Unpaid Tax	£420	Go to note 5
Total tax-free amount	£1,632	

Your total tax-free amount is used as follows	Tax code	For help
BROADWOOD ENGINEERS LTD £1,702 of this income is tax-free	163 L	Go to note 6
This totals your tax-free amount £1,702		Go to note 7

SOURCE HMRC

On the first line of the Notice is Simon's personal allowance for 2021/22 of £12,570. The amounts taken away from Simon's allowances are on the lines below. These are as follows.

- The first three deductions are the taxable figures of the benefits-in-kind of a company car, free fuel for private motoring and private medical insurance cover provided to Simon and his family by his employer. The Income Tax payable by Simon on these benefits is, therefore, collected by restricting his allowances by the taxable amount of the benefits.

- The last deduction is for tax of £84.00 underpaid in 2019/20. For a number of reasons the allowances given, or deductions included, in Simon's Notice of Coding may turn out not to be totally correct. If, as a result, tax is underpaid, this is usually collected in a subsequent year by restricting allowances in the coding. In the illustration a restriction of Simon's 2020/21 allowances by £420 will enable HMRC to collect the underpayment of £84.00 (£420 @ 20 per cent) from him.

The combined effect of these adjustments is to leave Simon with allowances of just £1,702 to be set against his salary for 2020/21. His code number is 163L. It is not difficult to see that there is a direct link between Simon's allowances and his code number. The suffix letter added to the coding is a way of identifying the category into which a taxpayer falls:

- C indicates you are a taxpayer resident in Wales.
- L is for a code with the basic personal allowance.
- M shows that you have received 10 per cent of your spouse's/partner's personal allowance.
- N tells you that you have transferred 10 per cent of your personal allowance.
- S applies if your main home is in Scotland.*
- OT means that:
  - your personal allowance has been used up;
  - you have started a new job and do not have a form P45; or
  - you fail to provide your new employer with the information needed to give you a tax code.
- T applies in many other cases, for example if:
  - your earnings exceed £100,000 resulting in a reduced personal allowance; or
  - there are items in the coding which need to be reviewed.

* There are five subsidiary tax codes dealing with the amount of tax to be deducted from the earnings of individuals liable to Scottish tax.

There are also a number of other codes.

- BR: this tells your employer to deduct tax at the basic rate.
- NT: no tax will be deducted.
- DO: tax will be deducted at the higher rate of 40 per cent.
- DI: tax will be taken off at the additional rate of 45 per cent.
- Prefix K: a K code is given to employees whose total deductions including taxable benefits exceed their personal allowances. The amount of the negative allowances is then added to the pay on which tax is payable. The system of K codes ensures that taxpayers pay all the tax due on their excess benefits evenly throughout the tax year under the PAYE system.
- X: this applies where HMRC will review the tax you have paid after 5 April.

Emergency tax codes

You may find that you are on an emergency tax code because you have:

- changed jobs;
- moved from self-employment to work for someone; or
- started receiving company benefits or the State Pension.

You will know if you are on an emergency tax code if the tax code on your payslip in 2021/22 is:

- 1250L WI;
- 1250L MI;
- 1250L X.

As a result you will pay Income Tax on all your earnings which exceed the 2021/22 personal allowance of £12,570.

An emergency tax code is only temporary. Your employer can help you get on the right tax code.

How tax is worked out using your tax code

The coding notice issued to Simon Black for 2021/22 tells him that his tax-free amount for the year is £1,630. He earns £43,680 per annum in his job.

The deduction for tax is worked out as follows:

	£
Pay from employment	43,680
Less: Tax-free amount for year	1,630
Tax due on	41,978
Income Tax payable	
£37,700 @ 20 per cent	7,540
£4,350 @ 40 per cent	1,740
	9,280

To work out the weekly amounts of pay and tax, divide the pay and tax payable for the year by 52:

- Weekly pay is £43,680 ÷ 52 = £840.00
- Weekly tax is £9,251 ÷ 52 = £177.90

To work out the equivalent monthly amount divide by 12:

- Monthly pay is £43,680 ÷ 12 = 3,640.00
- Monthly tax is £9,251 ÷ 12 = £770.91

Form P60

Shortly after the end of each tax year every employer sends HMRC a Return summarizing:

- the names of all employees;
- their earnings during that tax year; and
- the deductions made for both Income Tax and National Insurance Contributions.

By 31 May following the end of a tax year, your employer must give you your Form P60 on paper or electronically. This is a certificate of your earnings for the past tax year. It also shows:

- how much Income Tax and National Insurance Contributions you paid;
- the Code Number used in working out the deductions for Income Tax;
- your National Insurance number; and
- your employer's name and address.

Figure 5.2 is an illustration of the Form P60 sent to Anne Ford by her employer for 2021/22. This shows:

- the tax deducted from her earnings of £37,440 in the year amounted to £7,272, based on a tax code of 201L; and
- she made National Insurance Contributions totalling £3,456.96

Starting work

Your employer will ask you to fill in HMRC's new starter checklist if you:

- are starting a job for the first time;
- have not already been in work during the tax year;
- are also in another job; or
- receive the State Pension or an occupational pension.

The information on the new starter checklist enables your employer to:

- work out your tax code;
- set you up on their payroll software; and
- register you with HMRC.

As a result the right deductions for Income Tax and National Insurance can be made from your wage or salary.

Moving jobs

Whenever you change your job your old employer will give you Parts 1A, 2 and 3 of Form P45. On this form are:

- your name and address;

Figure 5.2   Form P60

P60 End of Year Certificate

Tax year to 5 April **2022**

To the employee:

Please keep this certificate in a safe place as **you will need it if you have to fill in a tax return. You also need it to make a claim for tax credits or to renew your claim.**

It also helps you check that your employer is using the correct National Insurance number and deducting the right rate of National Insurance contributions.

By law you are required to tell HM Revenue and Customs about any income that is not fully taxed, even if you are not sent a tax return.

HM Revenue and Customs

The figures marked ★ should be used for your tax return, if you get one

Employee's details

Surname	FORD
Forenames or initials	ANNE

National Insurance number: BZ 62 24 17A

Works/payroll number:

Pay and Income Tax details

	Pay		Tax deducted	
	£	p	£	p
In previous employment(s)				
				if refund mark 'R'
In this employment ★	37,440	00	8,443	00
Total for year	37,440	00	8,443	00

Final tax code: 201 L

National Insurance contributions in this employment

NIC table letter	Earnings at the Lower Earnings Limit (LEL) (where earnings are equal to or exceed the LEL) £	Earnings above the LEL, up to and including the Primary Threshold (PT) £	Earnings above the PT, up to and including the Upper Earnings Limit (UEL) £	Employee's contributions due on all earnings above the PT £	p
A	6,136	2,496	28,808	3,456	96

Statutory payments included in the pay In this employment figure above	Statutory Maternity Pay £ p	Statutory Paternity Pay £ p	Statutory Shared Parental Pay £ p
	Statutory Adoption Pay £ p		

Other details

Student Loan deductions in this employment (whole £s only) £

Your employer's full name and address (including postcode)

FORD ENGINEERS LTD
BRIDGE STREET
BROADWOOD
PT3 7GN

To employee

ANNE FORD
12 CHURCH RISE
BROADWOOD
PT3 8ZL

Employer PAYE reference: 28/B604

Certificate by Employer/Paying Office:
This form shows your total pay for Income Tax purposes in this employment for the year.
Any overtime, bonus, commission etc, Statutory Sick Pay, Statutory Maternity Pay, Statutory Paternity Pay, Statutory Shared Parental Pay or Statutory Adoption Pay is included.

SOURCE HMRC

- the name and address of your past employer;

- your tax district and reference number;

- your code number at the date of leaving;

- your accumulative salary and the tax deductions for the tax year up to the date that you leave; and

- your salary and tax deductions from the last employment unless this information is the same as the accumulative figures.

Your ex-employer submits the first part of the Form P45 to their tax district online.

Parts 2 and 3 of the Form P45 must be given:

- to your new employer; or

- Jobcentre Plus if you are not in work.

Your new employer will enter your address and the date you start your new job before sending Part 3 of the form to their own tax office. The information on the form allows your current employer to make the correct deductions for Income Tax and National Insurance from your salary or wage from the date you start your new job.

You should keep Part 1A of the form for your own records because it may be helpful when you come to prepare your own Tax Return.

Tax-deductible expenses

The rules allowing you to claim tax relief on expenses connected with your employment are extremely restricted. You are denied tax relief on almost all types of expense that are not ultimately borne by your employer. This is because, as an employee, you have to show that any expenditure is incurred 'wholly, exclusively and necessarily' in performing the duties of your employment. If your employer will not foot the bill for the expenditure involved, then HMRC take the view that it was incurred as a matter of choice rather than of necessity. Nevertheless, some business expenses paid personally are deductible from your income and should be claimed on your Tax Return.

Tax Saver

There are several tax-deductible expenses that can be used.

- Annual subscriptions to a professional body.

- Business use of your own car and telephone.

- Travel and overnight expenses.

- Clothing and upkeep of tools – HMRC and the trade unions have agreed flat-rate allowances for the upkeep of tools and special clothing in most classes of industry. The current rates are set out in Appendix 1. As an alternative you can claim a deduction for the actual amounts spent on these items.

- Payment by directors or employees for work-related insurance cover. Tax relief is also allowed on meeting the cost of uninsured liabilities.

Tax-free expenses

Tax Saver

The cost of most expenses you incur in your work is ultimately met by your employer, who either reimburses you on an expense claim or pays for them direct. There are several tax-free non-financial benefits for employees.

- Free or subsidized meals in a staff canteen, providing the facilities can be used by all staff.

- Sporting and recreational facilities.

- Staff parties, providing the annual cost to the employer is no more than £150 per head.

- Awards for long service of at least 20 years. The cost of the articles purchased by the employer must not exceed £50 for each year of service.

- Gifts not exceeding £250 in the tax year to an employee from a third party by reason of his or her employment.

- One routine health check and one medical screening each year.

- Eye tests and corrective glasses if your employer is required, by law, to provide eye and eyesight tests for you because of the work you do.

- Up to £500 each year for recommended medical treatment, so you can get back to work.

- Work-related training expenses including fees, travel, reasonable subsistence and the cost of any books.

- The cost of out-placement counselling and retraining courses for both full- and part-time employees.

- Payments not exceeding £500 in a tax year by your employer for pensions advice.

- Equipment or facilities provided to disabled people to enable them to carry out their jobs.

- Computer and other office equipment loaned to employees for business use only.

- One mobile telephone per employee for private use.

- Childcare facilities at the workplace or elsewhere (but not on domestic premises).

- Employer-supported childcare of up to £55 a week. For higher and additional rate taxpayers joining an employer's scheme after 5 April 2011 the relief is limited to £28 and £25 respectively. Employers can either contract with an approved child carer or provide childcare vouchers. (No longer available for new entrants.)

- Up to £4 per week paid to you by your employer for working at home as part of your employment contract. You are not required to produce any supporting evidence of the costs you incur.

- Accommodation and subsistence expenses when your duties require you to travel abroad. HMRC have published a list of benchmarks for use by your employer. Only payments in excess of the rates are taxable.

- Personal incidental expenses when you stay away from home overnight on business. The most common expenses covered are newspapers, telephone calls to home and laundry. The tax-free limits, including VAT, are £5 per night for stays anywhere in the United Kingdom and £10 per night elsewhere. Where these limits are exceeded the whole payment becomes payable – not the excess.

- Bicycle and cycling safety equipment made available to employees mainly to get them between home and work.

- Parking facilities for cars, motorcycles or bicycles at or near your place of work.

- A work bus service.

- The cost of a taxi fare when you have been working late and either public transport is no longer available or it would be unreasonable to expect you to use it at a late hour. Infrequent late working means working until at least 9.00 pm not more than 60 times in a tax year.

- The cost of electricity provided in workplace charging points for electric or plug-in hybrid cars and vans owned by employees.

- Mileage allowances where employees use their car, van, motorcycle or pedal cycle on business.

The tax-free rates laid down by HMRC for 2021/22 are:

Cars and vans	
• First 10,000 miles	45 p per mile
• Excess	25 p per mile
Motorcycles	24 p per mile
Bicycles	20 p per mile

Tax Saver

Employees are taxed on payments made by their employers over and above the rates in the table, but they can claim back and get tax relief on the difference where their employers pay them less than the permitted rate.

Employee travel

The cost of travelling between home and work is not allowable for tax purposes, other than for disabled employees who are given financial help by their employers with home-to-work travel on public transport or by some other means.

However, tax relief is allowed on all your business travel where your journey starts from either home or your permanent workplace. Where the full cost of a journey is not reimbursed by your employer, you can claim tax relief on the excess miles not paid for by your employer.

(a) Site-based workers

These are employees who work at a number of different places for periods of a few weeks or months at a time. Travelling expenses reimbursed to them are tax-free providing:

- the worker initially expects the posting not to exceed two years, and the stay actually does last for less than this time;
- there is no requirement for an employee to return to his or her permanent workplace when each site job comes to an end; and
- an employee's work on-site may be considered as a single continuous period even if he or she is occasionally moved off-site.

(b) Employees with areas

The geographical area covered by employees such as salespeople is treated as their permanent place of work. The following special rules apply.

- All travel within the area is eligible for tax relief.
- Where an employee lives outside his or her area, travel to the start of the area is classified as home-to-work travel and is taxable if paid for by the employer.
- The entire country is likely to be the area for any employee whose duties extend to servicing customers throughout the whole of the United Kingdom.

All travelling appointments of service engineers are treated as business travel qualifying for tax relief.

(c) More than one workplace

No tax relief is due for travel from home to either place of work for employees with more than one permanent place of location. It is HMRC's view that a workplace is likely to be considered as permanent if:

- an employee regularly performs 40 per cent or more of the duties of the employment there;
- customers, suppliers and others would expect to make contact with the employee there; and
- the employee has an office or desk and support services.

Home working

The global Covid-19 pandemic saw huge numbers of staff working from home. The coronavirus outbreak accelerated the numbers giving up the daily commute. Thankfully, modern technology has facilitated this trend.

Tax Saver

However, to get tax benefits, you must be able to demonstrate that you work from home as a necessity rather than by choice. If you satisfy this test you should be able to claim tax relief on:

- a proportion of your household costs such as heating, lighting, telephone and water (if any);
- use of your car, computer and tools for your employer's business; and
- other expenses you incur on stationery, books and professional subscriptions for the business.

Benefits-in-kind

Directors and employees are generally taxed on:

- the actual value of any employment-related benefits; and
- taxable expenses.

However, trivial benefits-in-kind costing no more than £50 each are tax exempt. These might include:

- flowers or chocolates to celebrate a marriage or birth of a baby; and
- seasonal gifts, such as a turkey or bottle of wine at Christmas.

There is an annual cap of £300 on these so-called trivial benefits provided to:

- directors or other officer holders of small companies; and
- members of their families and households.

Information about your expense payments and benefits-in-kind is supplied by your employer to your tax office each year on Form P11D. Your employer should give you a copy of this form by 6 July following the end of the tax year. It sets out your employer's calculations of your taxable payments and cash equivalents of benefits-in-kind. It is up to you to claim those that are not taxable. This should not cause you any problem where expenses such as travelling and entertaining have genuinely arisen from the performance of the duties of your employment.

There are set rules for calculating some benefits.

(a) Company cars

> ### Tax Saver
>
> For many employees the company car continues to be an important part of the remuneration package. The system of taxing company cars is geared towards encouraging the cleaner use of cars by linking the tax charge to the exhaust emission of the car.
>
> When the time comes for you to change your company car it will pay you to look into the carbon dioxide emission of the proposed replacement. As you will see from the following table you will save tax on your company car benefit by opting for a car with a lower approved CO_2 emission figure.

The tax charge is based on a percentage of the list price of a car (including qualifying accessories) but graduated according to the level of the car's carbon dioxide (CO_2) emissions. The minimum charge is 13 per cent of list price, increasing to a maximum of 37 per cent if CO_2 emissions are above the prescribed level.

In view of their higher emissions of pollutants, diesel cars are subject to a 4 per cent supplementary charge. However, even for diesel cars the maximum charge cannot exceed 37 per cent of a car's price.

Following a change in how it calculates emissions-related taxes in April 2020, the UK government is currently using two tax tables, depending on when your car was first made. Vehicles that were registered prior to 6 April 2020 have one set of rates and vehicles built after 6 April 2020 have a different set.

The car benefit charges for cars with an approved CO_2 emissions figure are as follows:

Company Car Tax BIK Rates (models registered *prior* to 6 April 2020)

Vehicle CO$_2$ (g/km)	Electric range (miles)	2020–21 BIK rate (%)		2021–22 BIK rate (%)		2022–23 BIK rate (%)	
		Petrol, Electric, RDE2 Diesel	Non-RDE2 Diesel	Petrol, Electric, RDE2 Diesel	Non-RDE2 Diesel	Petrol, Electric, RDE2 Diesel	Non-RDE2 Diesel
0		0		1		2	
1–50	130+	2		2		2	
1–50	70–129	5		5		5	
1–50	40–69	8		8		8	
1–50	30–39	12		12		12	
1–50	<30	14		14		14	
51–54		15		15		15	
55–59		16		16		16	
60–64		17		17		17	
65–69		18		18		18	
70–74		19		19		19	
75		20		20		20	
76–79		20	24	20	24	20	24
80–84		21	25	21	25	21	25
85–89		22	26	22	26	22	26
90–94		23	27	23	27	23	27
95–99		24	28	24	28	24	28
100–104		25	29	25	29	25	29
105–109		26	30	26	30	26	30
110–114		27	31	27	31	27	31
115–119		28	32	28	32	28	32
120–124		29	33	29	33	29	33
125–129		30	34	30	34	30	34
130–134		31	35	31	35	31	35
135–139		32	36	32	36	32	36
140–144		33	37	33	37	33	37
145–149		34	37	34	37	34	37
150–154		35	37	35	37	35	37
155–159		36	37	36	37	36	37
160+		37	37	37	37	37	37

Company Car Tax BIK Rates (models registered *after* 6 April 2020)

Vehicle CO$_2$ (g/km)	Electric range (miles)	2020–21 BIK rate (%)		2021–22 BIK rate (%)		2022–23 BIK rate (%)	
		Petrol, Electric, RDE2 Diesel	Non-RDE2 Diesel	Petrol, Electric, RDE2 Diesel	Non-RDE2 Diesel	Petrol, Electric, RDE2 Diesel	Non-RDE2 Diesel
0		0		1		2	
1–50	130+	0		1		2	
1–50	70–129	3		4		5	
1–50	40–69	6		7		8	
1–50	30–39	10		11		12	
1–50	<30	12		13		14	
51–54		13		14		15	
55–59		14		15		16	
60–64		15		16		17	
65–69		16		17		18	
70–74		17		18		19	
75–79		18	22	19	23	20	24
80–84		19	23	20	24	21	25
85–89		20	24	21	25	22	26
90–94		21	25	22	26	23	27
95–99		22	26	23	27	24	28
100–104		23	27	24	28	25	29
105–109		24	28	25	29	26	30
110–114		25	29	26	30	27	31
115–119		26	30	27	31	28	32
120–124		27	31	28	32	29	33
125–129		28	32	29	33	30	34
130–134		29	33	30	34	31	35
135–139		30	34	31	35	32	36
140–144		31	35	32	36	33	37
145–149		32	36	33	37	34	37
150–154		33	37	34	37	35	37
155–159		34	37	35	37	36	37
160–164		35	37	36	37	37	37
165–169		36	37	37	37	37	37
170+		37	37	37	37	37	37

Where the CO_2 figure for a car is not a multiple of 5, it is rounded down to the nearest 5.

The regime extends to all cars, not just new ones. However, special rules apply to:

- older cars (those registered before 1 January 1998); and
- cars first registered on or after 1 January 1998 with no CO_2 emissions.

Cars first registered before 1 January 1998 will have no CO_2 emissions figures and, therefore, the taxable car benefit is worked out on a percentage of list price based on engine size:

Engine size (cc)	Percentage of list price that is taxed
Up to 1,400	23
1,401–2,000	34
2,001 or more	37

The same applies to cars registered on or after 1 January 1998 with no CO_2 emissions figures, as follows:

Engine size (cc)	Percentage of list price that is taxed
Up to 1,400	20 (24 per cent if diesel)
1,401–2,000	31 (35 per cent if diesel)
2,001 or more	37
No cylinder capacity	37

A 13 per cent rate applies to all cars which cannot produce carbon dioxide when driven.

Tax Saver

Sometimes it is better to own your own car and charge your employer for the cost of all your business mileage. But you must keep a proper and detailed log of all business and private mileage.

Mileage between home and work counts as private, not business, usage except in a car made available to an employee who:

- has a travelling appointment;
- travels from home to a temporary place of work if the distance travelled is less than the distance between the normal place of work and the temporary place of work; or

- is a home worker and travels from home to another place of work in the performance of his or her duties.

There are several other circumstances where home-to-work travel in an employer-provided car is considered to be private use but is disregarded for tax purposes. These are where the car is provided:

- to a disabled person for home-to-work travel and there is no other private use;
- for home-to-work travel when public transport is disrupted; and
- for late-night journeys home from work.

(b) Fuel benefits

If your employer pays for fuel for your private motoring, this also gives rise to a taxable benefit on which you have to pay Income Tax. The taxable amount is calculated on the car benefit percentage for the CO_2 emissions of your car multiplied by 24,600, giving the following taxable benefits for the 2021/22 tax year:

CO_2 emissions (g/km)	Percentage of £24,600 that is taxed		Taxable benefit (£)	
	Petrol	Diesel	Petrol	Diesel
0–50	16	20	3,936	4,920
51–75	19	23	4,674	5,658
76–94	22	26	5,412	6,396
95	23	27	5,658	6,642
100	24	28	5,904	6,888
105	25	29	6,150	7,133
110	26	30	6,396	7,380
115	27	31	6,642	7,626
120	28	32	6,888	7,872
125	29	33	7,133	8,118
130	30	34	7,380	8,364
135	31	35	7,626	8,610
140	32	36	7,872	8,856
145	33	37	8,118	9,102
150	34	37	8,364	9,102

(continued)

(Continued)

155	35	37	8,610	9,102
160	36	37	8,856	9,102
165	37	37	9,102	9,102
170	37	37	9,102	9,102
175	37	37	9,102	9,102
180 and above	37	37	9,102	9,102

The benefit is:

- reduced to zero if the full cost of fuel for all your private motoring is reimbursed to your employer;
- proportionately reduced if you stop enjoying the use of free fuel for non-business motoring part way through a tax year; and
- not charged for any period of at least 30 days during which your car cannot be used or is unavailable to you.

Tax Saver

You will often be better off paying for your own fuel for non-business mileage.

(c) Company vans

If your employer provides you with a company van in 2021/22 without any unrestricted use, no matter the age or size of the van:

- you are taxed on a fixed amount of £3,500;
- for a company van with zero emission the benefit is 80 per cent of the fixed charge – this is equivalent to a taxable amount of £2,800;
- there is an additional benefit of £669 where your employer pays for fuel for private mileage.

(d) Pooled vehicles

The private use of a car from an employer's pool of vehicles will not give rise to a tax charge on an employee provided:

- any home-to-work travel is merely incidental to business use; and
- the vehicle is not garaged at or near the employee's home overnight.

(e) Living accommodation

In some trades it is established practice for an employer to provide living accommodation. This can also be desirable where there is a security risk. No Income Tax liability arises in either set of circumstances.

In other situations Income Tax is chargeable on the annual value of the property after deducting any rent paid for it. For these purposes the annual valuation is broadly equivalent to the gross rateable value. Estimated rateable values will be used for new properties not appearing on the domestic rating list.

An additional tax charge arises where the accommodation costs more than £75,000. This is worked out by applying HMRC's official interest rate (see below) to the excess of the cost price above £75,000.

(f) Beneficial loans

The rules dealing with interest-free or low-rate-interest loans from an employer are as follows:

- The taxable benefit is worked out by applying HMRC's official rate of interest to the loan, currently 2 per cent.
- Any interest actually paid on the loan reduces the amount of the benefit.
- No tax charge arises where all of an employee's cheap or interest-free loans, excluding loans that qualify for tax relief, total less than £10,000.
- There is no tax charge where the loan is for a purpose on which the interest would qualify for tax relief (see Chapter 4).

(g) Medical insurance

You will be taxed on the cost of private medical insurance premiums paid by your employer for you or other members of your family. Not subject to tax is the cost of medical insurance cover, or actual medical treatment overseas, while away on business.

(h) Relocation expenses

An employee who changes job, or is relocated by his or her employer, is not taxed on the costs of a relocation package up to £8,000. This limit applies to each job-related move. There are specific definitions for the removal expenses and benefits that qualify for exemption within the monetary limit.

Employee share ownership

There are a variety of share, profit sharing and share option schemes, all offering different investment limits and tax reliefs – some more generous than others. Membership of whatever scheme is operated by your employer and may be an attractive long-term investment with built-in tax advantages.

(a) Under a Share Incentive Plan

- Employers can give employees up to £3,600 of shares free of Income Tax and National Insurance.

- Some or all of these shares can be awarded to employees for reaching performance targets.

- Employees are able to buy partnership shares out of their pre-tax salary or wage up to a maximum of 10 per cent of salary or £1,800 a year, free of Income Tax and National Insurance.

- Employers can match partnership shares by giving employees up to two free shares for each partnership share they buy.

- Employees who sell their shares are liable to Capital Gains Tax only on any increase in the value of their shares after they come out of a plan.

- Free and matching shares must normally be kept in the plan for at least three years – employees can take partnership shares out of the plan at any time.

- Shares must come out of the plan when employees leave and some employees may lose their free and matching shares if they leave their jobs within three years of getting the shares.

- Dividends, up to £1,500 annually, paid on the shares are tax-free providing they are reinvested in additional shares in the company and retained for at least three years.

- Employees who keep their shares in a plan for five years pay no Income Tax or National Insurance on those shares.

- Employees who take their shares out of a plan after three years pay Income Tax and National Insurance on no more than the initial value of the shares – any increase in the value of their shares while in the plan is free of Income Tax and National Insurance.

- Capital Gains Tax roll-over relief is available for existing shareholders of smaller companies who want to sell their shares to a new plan trust to be used for the benefit of employees.

(b) The main features of a Savings-Related Share Option Scheme

- It operates in combination with either a bank or building society SAYE savings contract under which employees save a fixed regular amount each month.

- The maximum amount that can be saved is £500 per month over either a three- or five-year period.

- The price at which options can be offered to directors and employees cannot be less than 80 per cent of the market value of the shares at the time the options are granted.

- The receipt of the options and any increase in the value of the shares between the time that the options are granted and the date when they are exercised are free of Income Tax.

(c) Under an Approved Profit-Sharing Scheme

- A company makes an allocation of profits to trustees who, in turn, use the contribution in acquiring shares in the company that are subsequently allotted to employees.

- The limit on the market value of shares that may be appropriated to any one individual in each tax year is 10 per cent of salary, with a minimum limit of £3,000 and a maximum of £8,000.

- There is no Income Tax liability when the shares are set aside or if they are retained by the trustees of the scheme for three years.

(d) Inland Revenue Approved Share Option Plan

- No liability to Income Tax is imposed on a director or employee who acquires, or disposes of, ordinary shares under such a plan.

- The market value of shares, at the time of the grant of the option, over which an individual holds unexercised rights under the plan must not exceed £30,000.

- An option must be exercised not less than three, or more than 10, years after it is granted, or under three years after a previous exercise.

- The gain is measured by the difference between the sale proceeds and the cost of acquiring the shares, and is charged to Capital Gains Tax at the time of disposal.

- The price payable must be fixed at the time of the grant and must not be less than the market value of the shares at that date.

(e) Employee shareholder shares

- Employee shareholders are either issued or allotted shares worth a minimum of £2,000 in consideration of an employee shareholder agreement.

- For Income Tax purposes employee shareholders will be deemed to have paid £2,000 for their shares, thereby reducing the tax charge at the time of issue or allotment.

- You only pay Capital Gains Tax on gains in excess of £100,000 that you realize during your lifetime.

Enterprise Management Incentives

Enterprise Management Incentives are aimed at:

- helping small companies attract and retain the key people they need; and

- rewarding employees for taking a risk by investing their time and skills in helping small companies achieve their potential.

Normally, without any charge to Income Tax or National Insurance, companies can grant share options to employees worth up to £250,000 at the time of the grant.

A qualifying employee is one who must spend at least 25 hours a week, or if less, 75 per cent of his or her working time on the business of that company.

Payments on termination of employment

It is often the practice for an employee to be paid a lump sum on the termination of an employment, which can comprise any of the following:

- outstanding salary or wages;
- holiday pay;
- redundancy pay;
- a payment in lieu of notice; and
- compensation for loss of office.

Such payments, which are free of tax, are where:

- the employment ceases because of the accidental death, injury or disability of the employee; or
- most of the employee's time was spent working overseas for the employer.

Otherwise it is necessary to split the award between:

- income from the employment; and
- the remainder.

The amount to be treated as earnings is the 'post-employment notice pay', the calculation of which is not entirely straightforward.

Of the remainder:

- the first £30,000 (including any statutory or contractual redundancy pay) is tax-free; and
- the excess over £30,000 is taxable.

It is not unusual for redundancy and employment termination settlements to provide for benefits, such as membership of a company medical insurance scheme, to continue after the employment has come to an end. Such payments and benefits are taxed only to the extent that they actually arise, and in the year in which they are received or enjoyed.

Belinda Morrison was made redundant in May 2020. Under her employment termination settlement she received non-employment notice pay lump sum payments of £26,000 and £20,000 on 23 May 2020 and 9 April 2021 respectively. She was also permitted to retain her membership of her employer's company medical insurance scheme for four years at an annual cost to her employer of £1,000. Belinda's total redundancy package for 2020/21 comes to £27,000. As this is below the £30,000 exemption limit she does not pay tax on any part of the package she received in 2021/21. The balance of the exemption limit of £3,000 is carried forward to 2021/22 to be set against the cash payment of £20,000 and the medical insurance benefit of £1,000. For 2021/22, therefore, Belinda's old employer will deduct tax on £18,000.

06
Value Added Tax

Value Added Tax (VAT) is a system for taxing what people spend. It is also administered by HMRC. The National Advice Service (NAS) is the main contact point for businesses. The NAS telephone number is 0300 200 3700.

What is VAT?

VAT is a self-assessed tax charged on:

- the supply of goods and services in the United Kingdom; and
- the import of goods and certain services into the United Kingdom.

It applies where a taxable person in business makes supplies that are taxable supplies.

Rates of VAT

There are three rates of VAT: a standard rate of 20 per cent, a reduced rate of 5 per cent and a zero rate. Most of the goods and services supplied in the United Kingdom are liable to tax at the standard rate. Among the goods and services liable at the two lower rates are:

- Supplies charged at 5 per cent:
  - domestic fuel and power;
  - renovations and alterations of dwellings;
  - residential conversions;
  - car and booster seats for children; and
  - motorcycle and cycle helmets.

- Zero-rated supplies:
  - food sold in shops;
  - books, magazines and newspapers;
  - babywear;
  - children's clothing and footwear;
  - construction of new homes; and
  - passenger transport.

Exempt supplies

Some goods and services have no VAT on them. These include:

- education and training;
- health and welfare;
- insurance;
- land; and
- finance services and banking.

If you sell goods or supply services that are exempt:

- you do not charge VAT on your income; and
- you cannot recover VAT incurred on the purchases and expenses of your business.

Special rules apply where your business makes both chargeable and exempt supplies.

Registration

If you are just starting up a business it is unlikely you will need to register for VAT immediately. Only when the value of your taxable supplies reaches £85,000 in a 'rolling' 12-month period is it compulsory to apply for registration. HMRC have said that the VAT registration and deregistration thresholds will not change for two years from 1 April 2020. In working out the turnover of your business for this purpose, remember that taxable supplies are not just those liable at the standard rate but include supplies liable to tax at the lower rates of 5 per cent and zero.

You also need to register if the taxable supplies of your business in the next 30 days are likely to exceed the registration limit of £85,000. Also, do not delay making an application for registration if you acquire an existing business where the previous owner was VAT registered. Sometimes it is possible for you to take on the same registration number as that of the previous owner.

> Simon Potter started up in business in August 2018. He has been successful in building up his turnover each month. Looking back from the end of January 2021, his turnover for the previous 12 months was £81,000. But when he did the same exercise a month later this figure had increased to £87,000. Simon had to notify liability to register by 31 March 2021 and was registered for VAT from 1 April 2021.

You can apply for VAT registration by either:

- using HMRC's online services; or
- downloading Form VAT1 and sending the completed form in the post.

Applying online:

- is easier, faster and more secure;
- is certain as you get an immediate acknowledgement that your application has been received by HMRC; and
- allows you to access your certificate of registration through 'Your HMRC services' page.

When you register you will be sent a VAT registration certificate confirming:

- your VAT number;
- when you need to submit your VAT Return; and
- the date of your first payment.

It also shows your effective date of registration, which is:

- the date you went over the threshold; or
- the date from which you requested voluntary registration (see below).

Until you get your VAT number you must not charge, or show, VAT on your invoices. But you will still need to pay over the VAT to HMRC for this period.

> ## Tax Saver
>
> It is a good idea to put up your prices to allow for this. Just tell your customers the reason for the increase. When you know your VAT number you can then reissue the invoices detailing the VAT.

You can avoid registration:

- if your taxable turnover temporarily goes above the threshold for registration; and
- you can show evidence why you believe it will not exceed the de-registration threshold of £83,000 in the next year.

Voluntary registration

Sometimes there are benefits from VAT registration even though the turnover of your business is below the compulsory limit for registration. Voluntary registration is allowed providing you can show that you are, or will be, making some taxable supplies.

> ## Tax Saver
>
> An advantage of voluntary registration is that you can reduce your costs by recovering VAT incurred on your business expenses, including VAT paid on certain start-up costs and on the acquisition of assets such as computers and printers.

Voluntary registration is also beneficial where:

- customers will only deal with a supplier who is registered for VAT; or
- the image of your business will be enhanced.

But if your customers are the general public, voluntary registration is unlikely to be to your advantage. They cannot recover the VAT charged on your goods and services so you may be putting yourself at a price disadvantage compared to your competitors.

Cancellation of registration

You can apply to HMRC to de-register your business from VAT where the taxable turnover falls below the de-registration threshold of £83,000.

De-registration is compulsory where:

- you cease to trade; or
- you sell your business.

Help from HMRC

Telephone support is available on the VAT, Customs and Excise Helpline at 0300 200 3700. You can also get help with VAT by using videos, webinars, online courses and email updates from HMRC.

You should also find the VAT notices and leaflets published by HMRC useful in helping you understand and deal with VAT aspects of your business. Some of these, available from the NAS, are listed in Appendix 2.

VAT invoices

There is a lot of mandatory information you must show on all VAT invoices issued by your business, whether paper or electronic. This includes:

- the date of issue;
- a sequential number that uniquely identifies the invoice;
- your VAT identification number;
- the full name and address of both your own business and that of your customer;
- a description of the quantity and nature of the goods supplied or services rendered;
- the time of the supply;
- the net unit price;
- the gross amount payable, excluding VAT;
- the rate of VAT charged; and
- the amount of VAT payable.

There are also other specific requirements but these only apply in certain circumstances such as supplies to and from other EU countries.

Alternatively you can agree with your customers that they will raise the invoices for the goods or services you have supplied to them. This practice is known as self-billing.

Simplified and modified invoices can be issued for supplies of retail goods under, and over, £250 respectively.

Records, accounting and Returns

If your business is VAT registered you must:

- render tax invoices for all taxable supplies of goods and services;

- retain copies of all VAT invoices issued and received, filed in an orderly manner;

- maintain proper business and accounting records and keep them for at least six years;

- maintain an account showing the calculations of your VAT liability for each VAT period; and

- make timely VAT Returns and payments to HMRC.

The VAT payable, or repayable, each period is the simple difference between your VAT output tax and input tax. Output tax is what you charge on the goods and services (outputs) to your customers. Input tax is what you incur on the purchases and expenses (inputs) of running your business.

Totalling the VAT on your outputs and inputs each month should make it fairly straightforward to bring together the information you need to complete the VAT Return – Form VAT100 – for the accounting periods shown on your registration certificate.

Beth Way runs a hairdressing salon which is VAT registered. She has been given quarterly VAT accounting periods in line with the calendar quarters. She accounts for VAT as a retailer on the basis of the income received each quarter. Her VAT account for the three months to the end of March 2022 was:

	£	£
Output Tax		
January	1,940	
February	1,830	
March	2,070	
Total	5,840	5,840
Input Tax		
January	220	
February	160	
March	250	
Total	630	630
Net amount due to HMRC		5,210

The various boxes on your VAT Return can be filled in from the figures in your VAT account and the tax-exclusive values of your outputs and inputs for the period.

Make sure you submit each Return and pay what is due to HMRC within the stipulated time limit. If the VAT you have reclaimed on the purchases and expenses of the business exceeds the VAT on your turnover for the period, the Return will show you are entitled to a repayment, which will be sent direct to your bank account within 30 days of HMRC receiving your VAT Return.

If you wish, you can request that your quarterly VAT Return periods co-incide with your financial year.

Online filing of Returns

All businesses, irrespective of their turnover, must:

- file VAT Returns online; and
- pay any VAT due electronically.

There are a number of benefits from online filing such as up to an extra seven days to:

- file your Return; and
- pay any VAT due.

To pay by Direct Debit, the internet, telephone or BACS Direct Payment you need the following information:

Sort code: 08-32-00

Account number: 11963155

Account name: HMRC VAT

Quote your VAT registration number leaving no gaps.

You can always look at your VAT online account to find out if your payment is on your record. It should be updated within 48 hours of receipt.

When signing up for online filing you should have:

- provided an email address; and

- set up an email reminder. This will be the only communication to you from HMRC that it is now time to complete a Return.

Making VAT Digital

Making Tax Digital for VAT means that if your business has a taxable income above the requirement for VAT registration it must:

- keep records in digital form; and
- file the VAT Returns using software.

As a result the software which your business uses must be able to:

- keep and maintain the records set out in the covering regulations;
- prepare your VAT Returns using the information kept in these digital records; and
- communicate with HMRC digitally via the specific Interface platform.

These rules apply for your first VAT period starting on or after 1 April 2019.

Input tax

The actual amount of input tax on purchases does not matter quite so much when the Flat Rate Scheme is used (see page 82). For other businesses it is only the input tax on the costs of the business that can be claimed when VAT

Returns are completed. Sometimes expenses may be incurred where input tax cannot be claimed at all. Examples are:

- business entertaining; and
- private purchases paid for through your business.

Occasionally there may be a need to apportion input tax, such as that on home telephone bills incurred partly for business and partly for private purposes. Apportionment is best done on a percentage basis which, provided it is reasonable, HMRC can be expected to accept.

Tax Saver

You can also recover VAT paid on certain purchases made by your business before it was registered for VAT. But there is a time limit for back-dating claims, which is:

- four years for goods you still own, or which were used in making other goods you still have; and
- six months for services.

The goods and services:

- must relate to the purpose of the business; and
- you can reclaim the VAT on them on your first VAT Return.

Motor cars and fuel

Businesses directly concerned with motoring, such as new car dealers, vehicle hirers, taxi drivers or driving schools, may be able to reclaim all input tax on cars that they buy or lease. Input tax cannot be claimed back on cars bought by other businesses and made available for private use. However, it may be possible to claim 50 per cent of the input tax on the rental payments where cars are leased.

There are two alternative methods for dealing with input tax on motor fuel, namely:

- all input tax is claimed and a fixed-scale charge to take account of private use is applied. From 1 May 2020 the fuel scale charges, based on a 20 per cent rate, for a three-month period are as follows; and

- no input tax is claimed and the fixed-scale charge is ignored. If you intend to deal with motor fuel this way you should write to HMRC to tell them.

Input tax on repairs and maintenance of business cars can be claimed whichever way you decide to deal with motor fuel.

Quarterly scale charges for 2021/22

CO_2 emissions in g/km	Quarterly Scale Charge (£)	VAT due (£)
120 or below	145	24.17
125	219	36.50
130	233	38.83
135	247	41.17
140	262	43.67
145	277	46.17
150	292	48.67
155	306	51.00
160	321	53.50
165	336	56.00
170	350	58.33
175	364	60.67
180	379	63.17
185	394	65.67
190	409	68.17
195	423	70.50
200	438	73.00
205	453	75.50
210	467	77.83
215	481	80.17
220	496	82.67
225 and above	511	85.17

Bad debts

Late or non-payment of bills can often have a serious impact on both the cashflow and profitability of a business. When it comes to bad debts it is only when a debt is more than six months old (from the date the payment was due) that an adjustment can be made to recover VAT accounted for on that debt in a previous VAT Return. The debt must be less than four years and six months old.

Adjustments for bad debts, although not separately shown on VAT Returns, must be recorded separately in the VAT account of your business. Listings must be maintained to support both the entries and any further adjustments made to reflect subsequent amounts recovered.

All this information must be retained for four years.

Special schemes for retailers

Retailers often sell a mixture of both positive and zero-rated goods but do not know how much of each of them is sold from day to day. When this happens they can use one of the schemes available to help them work out their VAT liabilities. If you are in retailing, you should study the leaflets telling you about the various schemes so that you do not pay too much tax.

Where retailers only sell goods that are liable at the standard rate of 20 per cent, the amount of tax included in the gross takings for a period is 1/6. Referred to as the 'VAT fraction', this calculation is worked out as follows:

	£
Tax-exclusive value (say)	100
Add: VAT @ 20 per cent	20
Tax-inclusive price	120
The VAT included in the tax-inclusive price is therefore	$\left(\dfrac{20}{120}\right)=\left(\dfrac{1}{6}\right)$

For goods liable at the reduced rate of 5 per cent the 'VAT fraction' is 1/21.

Flat Rate Scheme

Tax Saver

The scheme is open to small businesses whose annual taxable turnover (not including VAT) does not exceed £150,000. It will be of particular appeal to businesses that do not want to spend too much time and effort dealing with all the administrative complications of normal VAT accounting.

Under the scheme, VAT is still charged to customers at the rate appropriate to the supplies made by the business. When you come to complete your VAT Returns:

- you do not make a separate claim to recover input tax on purchases, expenses or low-value assets acquired for your business;
- input tax on a single purchase of a capital asset with a value of more than £2,000, including VAT, can be separately recovered; and
- you work out the tax due by applying a fixed percentage to the VAT inclusive turnover of your business for the period.

The percentages have been set by HMRC according to the principal activity of a business and take into account that input tax on normal purchases is not claimed.

Yvonne Spencer is a hairdresser. Her VAT inclusive turnover for the quarter to the end of March 2022 was £18,000. Yvonne must pay VAT of £2,340 as follows:

$$£18,000 \times 13 \text{ per cent} = £2,340$$

Businesses are being strongly encouraged by HMRC to use the scheme, so much so that a 1 per cent reduction in the percentages for the first year is available to new businesses:

- that register for VAT when they should; and
- apply to use the scheme at the same time.

You have to leave the scheme once the regular annual turnover of your business reaches a VAT inclusive amount of £230,000.

Cash accounting

Under the cash accounting scheme:

- you account for VAT on your outputs when you are paid for sales made by your business, rather than by reference to the date of your tax invoices; and

- you reclaim the VAT on your purchases and business expenses when you pay for them.

Your business is eligible to use this scheme from the beginning of a VAT tax period if:

- you expect the value of your taxable supplies (excluding VAT) during the forthcoming year to be no more than £1.35 million; and

- you are not in arrears in submitting past VAT Returns at the time you decide to join the scheme.

You must come out of cash accounting if:

- the amount of your taxable supplies exceeds £1.6 million (exclusive of VAT) in a period of one year; or

- your business fails to comply with the correct requirements for record keeping.

Annual accounting

Under the annual accounting scheme your business:

- submits just one VAT Return each year;
- makes interim payments of VAT based on an estimate of your liability for the year;
- completes and sends in its VAT Return two months after the end of the year. At the same time you pay over the balance of VAT due; and
- can use it together with both the cash accounting and flat rate schemes.

You can apply online to use the scheme if you reasonably believe that the amount of your taxable supplies, excluding VAT, in the period of 12 months from the date of your application will not exceed £1.35 million. If you are accepted onto the scheme, the start date for the new arrangements will be the first day of your current accounting period. You will be notified in writing if your application has been accepted. The letter you receive will also tell you:

- the amount and timing of your interim payments; and
- the due date of the Annual Return and balancing payment.

> Vince Charles is in business as a vehicle repairer and is registered for VAT. In October 2021 he applies to use the annual accounting scheme. His quarterly period runs from 1 September to 30 November. His first annual accounting period starts on 1 September 2021 and ends on 31 August 2022.

Once you are in the scheme you can remain in it until your annual turnover exceeds £1.6 million. You will then be taken off the scheme at the end of your current accounting year. Alternatively, if you want to come out of the scheme and go back to the normal method of paying and accounting for VAT you just need to tell HMRC of your decision.

VAT visits and inspections

VAT officers:

- can visit your business to look at your VAT records; and
- make sure that you are paying or reclaiming the correct amount of VAT.

HMRC usually contact you to arrange a visit and let you know:

- what information they want to look at;
- how long the visit should take; and
- whether they need to inspect your premises.

They normally give you seven days' notice. Afterwards you will get a letter from HMRC about:

- what, if anything, you must do to improve your records for VAT;
- any amendments you must make to your VAT account;
- under or over payments of VAT; and
- any penalty you need to pay.

Penalties, surcharges and interest

The penalty regime covering VAT aspects of your business extends to:

- failing to register for VAT on time; and
- errors in documents or Returns.

Penalties are calculated:

- as a percentage of the additional tax due; and
- when the inaccuracy is put right.

The penalty is a percentage of the extra tax due and depends on the reason for the inaccuracy as follows:

	Rate of penalty	
Reason	Maximum	Minimum
Reasonable care	30%	No Penalty
Deliberate	70%	20%
Deliberate and concealed	100%	30%

As you can see there is a substantial difference between the minimum and maximum rates of penalty. Therefore, even if you have adjusted for any error on the next VAT Return after it was identified, you should also:

- disclose the error with full details by writing to HMRC before it is picked up by them;
- help HMRC calculate the extra VAT due; and
- allow HMRC to look at any records requested to check on the accuracy of the figures.

By doing all of this you should be able to secure a much reduced level of penalty.

Where a disclosure is made following a prompt from HMRC, the minimum levels of penalty are increased as follows:

	Rate
Carelessness	10%/20%*
Deliberate	35%
Deliberate and concealed	50%

*Depending on whether the non-deliberate event took place within or after 12 months of the tax being due.

Furthermore:

- default interest, currently at a rate of 2.75 per cent, will normally be charged when assessments for errors are issued;

- surcharges can be imposed by HMRC where you fail to:
  - file your VAT Returns on time; and/or
  - pay the proper amount of tax when it is due.

Default surcharges:

- range from 2 per cent to 15 per cent where a history of default has built up;
- are subject to a minimum surcharge of £30; and
- at the 2 per cent and 5 per cent rates are seldom assessed unless they are calculated to exceed £400.

HMRC will pay you interest in cases where they make an official error but this is currently at the rate of 0.5 per cent.

Appeals

You have the right to appeal to an independent tribunal against:

- the imposition of a penalty;
- the amount of a penalty; and
- a decision not to suspend a penalty.

Alternatively you can opt for an internal review by an independent HMRC officer. This is a quick and inexpensive way to resolve any dispute.

Complaints

VAT officers are committed to the same standards as Tax staff (see the Service Commitment reproduced in Chapter 1), and are expected to abide by them. If you ever feel dissatisfied with the manner in which the affairs of your business have been handled, or think that an officer has overstepped the mark and has exceeded his or her authority, you can write to:

- the person who is in overall charge at the HMRC office for your business; or
- the Complaints Unit for the area where your business is situated.

If you are unable to resolve your complaint satisfactorily your next step is to contact the Adjudicator's Office, which is the independent body set up specifically for this purpose.

07
Working for yourself

If you run your own business, other than through a company or in partnership, you are classified as self-employed for tax purposes. Your business might be a trade, profession or vocation.

Am I self-employed?

The main distinguishing factor between having self-employed status and working as an employee is the existence of a 'master–servant' relationship. Sometimes it is difficult to draw a line between:

- employment (a contract for service); and
- self-employment (a contract for services).

Your business will have the trappings of self-employment if you:

- are responsible for the success or failure of your business;
- are paid a fixed fee, or price for your work;
- have several customers at the same time;
- can hire other people at your own expense to help you or to do the work for you;
- can decide how, when and where the work should be undertaken;
- can dictate the hours you work;
- provide your own tools; and
- have no entitlement to paid holidays or sick leave.

You do not have to formalize any business relationship by entering into a contract for the supply of goods or services. Nevertheless, having a contract makes sound business sense because it will cover matters other than those just relative to the taxation consequences of the relationship.

Starting up in business

Your business is now up and running. It is important that you quickly learn what to do about Tax, National Insurance (see Chapter 8) and maybe Value Added Tax (see Chapter 6).

I suggest you use the online tax registration service to tell HMRC about your new business. You will find this at http://www.gov.uk/new-business-register-for-tax. As part of the registration process you will be asked if you would like to receive business advisory emails. HMRC recognizes that starting and running a business is challenging. By signing up for this free service you will receive a series of tax-related help and support emails.

Other useful services offered by HMRC include:

- free online webinar presentations allowing you to attend seminars without leaving your desk;
- e-learning which you can use whenever it suits you, allowing you to learn at your own pace; and
- videos on HMRC's YouTube pages.

Records

It is strongly recommended that a separate bank account is maintained for all business income, purchases and expenses. As a minimum you should keep the following records, either electronically or manually:

- a cash book to record and analyze sales and other receipts, purchases and overhead expenses that pass through the bank account; and
- a petty cash book to log all small transactions paid for in cash.

If you run a larger business, you will probably need to maintain other accounting information as well.

Tax Saver

Whatever the size of your business it is a good discipline to:

- write up all your books of account on a regular basis; and
- maintain proper and accurate accounting records at all times.

Furthermore, in order to comply with the requirements for Self Assessment, you should keep and file the following:

- invoices for sales made by your business;
- bank statements and paying-in slips to show where the income comes from;
- invoices for goods acquired or costs incurred;
- documentation supporting purchases and sales of assets used in your business; and
- records in support of amounts taken out of the business for personal use (drawings) and all money paid into your business from personal funds (capital introduced).

Accounts

You can choose the date to which you draw up the accounts of your self-employment each year. For this reason it is unlikely that the first accounts will cover a full year of the activities of your business. You can make up your accounts from the date you start in business to the end of:

- a particular month;
- your first year's trading;
- the calendar year on 31 December; or
- the tax year.

Tax Saver

You should certainly think about your choice of accounting date. An obvious and convenient choice is 31 March as the date coincides with the end of the tax year on 5 April. However, it is sometimes preferable to go with the date early on in the tax year, such as 30 April, as it allows you more time to plan for the funding of the tax payable on your business profits.

Alternatively, if your business is seasonal in nature, it may be a good idea to pick an annual accounting date to coincide with the slack time of the year and when stocks are low.

Thereafter you should continue to draw up your accounts to the same date every year. You are allowed to change this date where you can show good reason to do so.

Your accounts should be drawn up to:

- work out the profit earned or loss sustained in the financial period; and
- summarize, whenever possible, on the balance sheet the amounts of the assets and liabilities at the year-end.

The statement of the profit or loss of your business is not usually the simple difference between receipts and payments. For example, if you sell to customers on credit there will inevitably be some unpaid sales at the year-end. These outstanding invoices need to come into your accounts as income for that period. Equally, where amounts are due to your suppliers for purchases or expenses at the end of your financial period these need to be included in the accounts as costs incurred in the period. If your business is:

- one that requires you to keep a stock of raw materials or finished goods, the value of that stock at the year-end must be included in the profit and loss statement as income. The basis of valuation is cost or, in the case of redundant or old stock, realizable value. The amount of your stock at the beginning of the accounting period is deductible as a cost; or
- of a professional nature or you are a service provider you must also make an adjustment to your accounts at the end of each accounting period. You must bring in as income an amount in respect of ongoing, but unbilled, work by reference to the proportion of the work completed.

When it comes to expenses make sure you claim all the overhead costs. For example:

Tax Saver

If you are married or live with a partner and your spouse/partner helps you in the business by doing your accounts and acting as a part-time secretary or assistant, you can claim the salary paid to him/her as a business expense. You should pay a proper amount for these services. If this is his or her only job or income and the wage is less than £9,500 for the year, then there will be no tax or National Insurance to pay.

Tax Saver

If you work from home you can claim a deduction for an appropriate proportion of the fixed costs of running your home, such as:

- mortgage interest;
- council tax;
- light, heat and household insurance;
- the rental of your landline telephone;
- broadband;
- general repairs and maintenance; and
- cleaning expenses.

In order to be eligible you must have a specific area in your home set aside as an office.

Tax Saver

There will be some costs of your business, such as a car used both privately and for work, when it may be difficult to apportion the expenditure between the private and business elements. Where there is this overlap, I suggest you include a note in the additional information section of the self-employed pages of your Tax Return, so your tax office can see how you have worked out the percentage of the expenditure chargeable to the business.

Tax Saver

Finally, avoid using estimates for any business expenses. If they are challenged on enquiry from HMRC you will find it difficult to substantiate what you have claimed in your accounts.

Jack Wagstaff has been in business for many years running the newsagents and confectionery shop in his local high street. He has three part-time assistants to help him in the shop.

His wife, Emily, looks after all the records of the business, pays the suppliers and completes the quarterly VAT Returns.

Jack makes up his accounts to 31 March each year. The statement of his business income and the expenses incurred during the year to 31 March 2021 are as follows:

		£	£	£
Sales				182,650
Less:	Cost of sales			
	Stock of cards, sweets, stationery, cigarettes etc at start of year		2,680	
	Purchases in the year		61,440	
			64,120	
Less:	Stock at end of year		3,240	60,880
Gross profit				121,770
Less:	Overhead expenses			
	Wages of part-time assistants	20,400		
	Wife's salary	6,200	26,600	
	Shop expenses			
	Rent	22,000		
	Business and Water Rates	13,750		
	Light and Heat	3,800		
	Insurance	820		
	Cleaning	1,560		
	Shop door repairs	620	42,550	
	Printing, postage and stationery		1,660	
	Shop telephone and fax		1,790	
	Computer costs		860	

(*continued*)

(Continued)

Entertaining		220
Accountancy		1,340
Legal fees re new lease		1,260
Car expenses		
Road Fund Licence and insurance	720	
Petrol and oil	1,720	
Repairs and servicing	530	2,970
Use of home as office (1/6 × £2,730)		455
Home telephone		820
Bank interest and charges		1,140
Staff welfare		390
Miscellaneous expenses		240	82,295
Profit for the year		39,475

Nowadays, annual accounts of a business are often needed for reasons other than tax. For example:

- to verify income in support of an application for a mortgage; or
- by your bank manager when weighing up an application for a business loan or overdraft facility.

Cash accounting for businesses

Alternatively, business owners can work out their annual taxable profit or loss by simply deducting monies paid for supplies or expenses from income received. They do not have to make adjustments for:

- stock or work-in-progress;
- unpaid bills for either purchases or overhead expenses; or
- outstanding invoices due from customers.

The scheme is:

- optional; and

- open to all traders or professionals whose annual income does not exceed £150,000.

You can elect to adopt the cash basis for 2021/22 by ticking box 10 on page SEF1 of your Tax Return.

You will have to come out of the cash basis for the year following that in which the receipts of your business are more than £300,000.

Some of the other features of the cash basis are:

- adjustments are required when coming or going out of the scheme to make sure that only once:

  - is income taxed; and

  - payments are deducted.

- payments for interest up to £500 each year are allowed. It does not matter whether the interest is on a loan for either business or private purposes; and

- monies spent on buying plant and machinery, but not cars, are deductable against income of the business.

Tax Saver

Losses incurred can be carried forward to be set against profits of future years. However, losses cannot be carried back or set off against other income. This restriction on tax relief for losses could be a significant disadvantage to some businesses.

Fixed-rate deduction scheme

You can also use optional simplified flat rate calculations to work out some of your business expenses. The main types of expenditure covered are those relating to cars, vans or motorcycles, and the use of your home. For each vehicle the costs included in the fixed deduction cover both the purchase and all running costs. Once the fixed-rate scheme has been used for a vehicle it is compulsory for each subsequent period that the vehicle is used in the business. The allowable rates for 2021/22 are:

	For each of the first 10,000 business miles	For each business mile over 10,000
Cars and goods vehicles	45 p	25 p
Motorcycles	24 p	24 p

For use of your home, you can deduct a fixed monthly rate which depends on the number of hours you, or any of your employees, spend working at your home. The monthly rates of deduction for 2021/22 are:

Number of hours worked per month	Allowable amount
25 to 50	£10
51 to 100	£18
101 or more	£26

However, this flat rate does not include the proportion of your telephone or internet used for your business. You can claim these expenses by working out the actual costs incurred.

Small business income allowance

There is a tax-free allowance of £1,000 for individuals:

- whose income from selling goods or providing services is small; and
- which will provide certainty regarding the tax obligations for the growing number of 'micro-entrepreneurs' such as occasional eBay sellers.

There is no reporting requirement where gross income is below £1,000. If income exceeds this threshold you can choose to either:

- claim expenses in the usual way; or
- simply deduct the allowance from gross income and ignore expenses.

You can decide which method to adopt on a year-by-year basis.

Tax Return information

If you were in business at any time during the 2021/22 tax year you will need to complete the supplementary self-employment pages to accompany your Tax Return for the year. The self-employment pages are in a set format for reporting the annual income and expenses of your business. Your Return will not be accepted as complete if the information about your business income and expenses is not presented in the required format.

When Jack Wagstaff comes to complete the supplementary self-employment pages for the year ended 5 April 2022 he will fill in the section on business income and expenses, based on his accounts for the financial year to 31 March 2022, as follows:

	£
Sales/business income (excluding VAT)	182,650
Expenses	
Cost of goods bought for re-sale or goods used	60,880
Payments to subcontractors	–
Wages, salaries and other staff costs	26,600
Car, van and travel expenses	2,970
Rent, rates, power and insurance costs	40,825
Repairs and renewals of property and equipment	620
Telephone, fax, stationery and other office costs	5,830
Advertising and business entertainment costs	220
Interest on bank and other loans	1,140
Bank, credit card and other financial charges	–
Irrecoverable debts written off	–
Accountancy, legal and other professional fees	2,600
Other finance charges	–
Depreciation and loss/(profit) on sale of assets	–
Other business expenses	1,490
Total expenses	**143,175**
Net profit	**39,475**

(*continued*)

(Continued)

Notes

(1) Wages, salaries and other staff costs

Part-time assistants	20,400
Wife's salary	6,200
	26,600

(2) Rent rates, power and insurance costs

Shop expenses (excluding cleaning and door repairs)	40,370
Use of home as office	455
	40,825

(3) Telephone, fax, stationery and other office costs

Printing, postage and stationery	1,660
Telephone (shop and home)	2,610
Shop cleaning	1,560
	5,830

(4) Accountancy, legal and other professional costs

Accountancy	1,340
Legal fees	1,260
	2,600

(5) Other business expenses

Computer costs	860
Staff welfare	390
Miscellaneous expenses	240
	1,490

So as to minimize the risk of HMRC raising enquiries into your self-employment income and Tax Return, you should adopt a consistent pattern from year to year in the way you analyse your business expenses under the various headings of the standardized format.

If the annual turnover of your business was below £85,000:

- you only need to complete the self-employment (short) supplementary pages; and

- you can add up all your business expenses allowable for tax purposes and just enter the total figure in Box 20 on page SES1.

Profits for tax

The profit disclosed by your business accounts will not necessarily be the same as that on which your tax bill is calculated. This is because certain types of expenditure are specifically not allowable in working out taxable business profits. These include:

- goods or materials bought for personal use;
- the private proportion of mixed expenses;
- business entertainment;
- non-business charitable donations;
- amounts spent on items of a capital nature;
- professional costs related to capital expenditure, such as the legal expenses of buying property;
- own wages or drawings; and
- general provisions and reserves.

Although Jack Wagstaff's accounts for his financial year to 31 March 2022 show he made a profit of £39,475, his taxable profit is £43,311 as follows:

	£	£
Profit as per accounts		39,475
Add: Disallowable expenses		
Private proportion of car expenses (60 per cent)	1,782	
Private proportion of home telephone (70 per cent)	574	
Entertainment	220	
Legal fees re new lease	1,260	
		3,836
Profit as adjusted for tax purposes		43,311

Profits of the tax year

Self-employed individuals are taxed on the profits of their financial year ending in the tax year. This is known as 'the basis period'.

> The tax-adjusted profit of £43,311 for the year to 31 March 2022 of Jack Wagstaff's high-street business will be taxed in 2021/22

There are special rules for working out the profits on which you pay tax in the opening years of your business, as follows:

- in the first tax year your taxable profits are those arising in the period from commencement to the following 5 April;
- if you choose to prepare your business accounts up to a date 12 months after you began your business then, in the second tax year, you pay tax on the profits for the first full year of trading; and
- for the third and all subsequent tax years you pay tax on the profits for 'the basis period'.

Under these rules it is usual for the profits for some periods of account to be taken into account more than once in working out the amount on which you pay tax. However, over the lifetime of your business it is intended that the profits should be taxed in full but once and once only. As a result, profits that are taxed more than once are eligible for a special relief. Known as overlap relief it will be given when either:

- a business ceases; or
- for any earlier tax year where the basis period exceeds 12 months.

> James Gray started up in business on 1 May 2019. His annual accounting date is 30 April. He makes the following profits in the first two years:
>
> Year to 30/04/2020   £24,720
>
> Year to 30/04/2021   £28,360

The taxable profits for the first three tax years are:

Tax year	Basis period	Taxable profit (£)
2019/20	01/05/2019 to 05/04/2020	22,660
2020/21	Year to 30/04/2020	24,720
2021/22	Year to 30/04/2021	28,360

On cessation the taxable profits for the final tax year will be those earned in the period from the end of the basis period in the previous tax year up to cessation, but reduced by overlap relief.

James Gray decides to close down his business on 30 April 2026. In the final year James makes profits of £34,950. The final tax year is 2026/27 and James will pay tax on:

	£
Taxable profit of final year	34,950
Less: Overlap, 01/05/2019 to 05/04/2020	22,660
Net taxable amount	12,290

Special rules apply when a business changes its accounting date. Apart from the first and last years of business, the profits of a 12-month period are taxed in each tax year.

Sheila Windows began her business on 1 December 2019. She draws up her first accounts to 30 November 2020 and makes a profit of £33,000. She then decides to change her accounting date by extending it to 31 January 2022. The accounts for this 14-month period show a taxable profit of £28,000. Her basis period and taxable profits for the opening years of the business are:

Tax year	Basis period	Taxable profit (£)
2019/20	01/12/2019 to 05/04/2020	11,000
2020/21	Year to 30/11/2019	33,000
The overlap period is from 01/12/2019 to 05/04/2020		
2021/22	01/12/2020 to 31/01/2022 (14 months)	28,000
Less: Overlap	01/12/2019 to 31/01/2020	5,500
Net taxable amount		22,500

The overlap period was one of four months. As the accounting period from 1 December 2020 to 31 January 2022 is 14 months, the overlap is a period of two months. The amount deducted from the taxable profits for 2021/22 is half of the original overlap profit. A further two months of overlap relief is available either when the business ceases or in any subsequent tax year when the basis period is again longer than 12 months.

Pre-trading and post-cessation expenses

Any expenditure which you incurred in the seven years before you started to trade is:

- treated as if it was spent on the first day of business; and
- tax deductible.

The relief only extends to those costs and other outgoings which would qualify for tax relief had they been incurred on the first day of trading.

Tax relief is also allowed on certain expenditure incurred after your business has ceased. The expenses that qualify for relief are:

- those closely related to the trading or professional activities previously carried on; and
- including, for example, relief for debts that have subsequently proved to be irrecoverable.

Relief is available for payments made within seven years of the permanent discontinuance of the business by setting the payments made against income for the same tax year. Any excess can be treated as a capital loss, but only of the same tax year.

Capital allowances

You can claim what are known as capital allowances on the expenditure you incur on items of a capital nature for your business.

Amounts spent by businesses attract the following rates of allowance in the first year:

- 100 per cent on annual expenditure up to £1 million* on most types of plant and machinery;

- 100 per cent on most energy-saving or environmentally beneficial plant and machinery;

- 100 per cent for purchases of new low-emission cars for use by you or your staff in your business (to qualify a car must not emit more than 50 g/km CO_2 or be electrically propelled);

- 100 per cent on the purchase of new electric vans; and

- 18 per cent for cars with CO_2 emissions above 50 g/km but not exceeding 110 g/km (this rate reduces to 8 per cent for cars exceeding this CO_2 emission limit).

* This limit took effect on 1 January 2019 for a period of two years. Previously it was £200,000.

> ## Tax Saver
>
> It may be tax efficient to incur capital expenditure towards the end of an accounting year rather than early in the following year. You will then benefit from any of the above first year allowances due on the expenditure at an earlier date.

In subsequent years your capital expenditure, after deducting your first year allowances, is further written down on the reducing-balance basis.

A separate 'pool' must be maintained for expenditure in each of the following different categories:

- all plant and equipment, including motor vans, lorries and cars with CO_2 emissions of 110 g/km* or less;
- all cars with CO_2 emissions exceeding 160 g/km;
- each asset where there is both business and personal use; and
- each asset with a short life expectancy.

The rates of allowance are:

- 18 per cent per annum; or
- 8 per cent per annum for cars purchased from 6 April 2009 onwards and with CO_2 emissions exceeding 110 g/km*.

*160 g/km for purchases before 6 April 2013, reducing to 130g/km for purchases between 6 April 2013 and 5 April 2018.

Where the unrelieved expenditure is no more than £1,000 you can claim tax relief on the full amount.

Where an asset on which capital allowances have been claimed is sold, you must bring the proceeds of sale into the computation of capital allowances. If it is sold for less than the value to which it has been written down for tax purposes you will probably be entitled to a further allowance equivalent to the difference between the sale proceeds and the written-down value.

These adjustments are respectively known as balancing allowances and balancing charges.

In his accounting year to 31 March 2022 Jack Wagstaff traded in his old car for £2,400 and bought a new one with a CO_2 emission limit of 100 g/km for £20,000. In the year he also spent £3,100 on fittings for his shop, £1,400 on a computer and printer and £200 on a new office filing cabinet. His claim to capital allowances for 2021/22, based on his capital expenditure in this year, is:

	(£)	Pool (£)	Car with private use (£)
Written-down values brought forward from 2018/19		6,300	4,100
Sale proceeds of car			2,400
Balancing allowance			1,700
Additions in the year			
Shop fittings, computer and cabinet		4,700	
New car			20,000
		11,000	
Allowances due			
Annual Investment – 100 per cent	4,700		
Writing down – 18 per cent	1,134	5,834	3,600
Carried forward to 2020/21		5,166	16,400
Summary of allowances			
Annual Investment		4,700	
Writing down		4,734	
Balancing		1,700	
		11,134	
Less: 60 per cent private use of car		3,180	
2021/22 Capital allowances		7,954	

Capital allowances are deducted from your profits as a trading expense of your business. Any balancing charges are treated as an addition to your profit. It follows that:

- the chargeable period for the purposes of working out your capital allowances is the same as that for which you draw up your accounts; and
- the length of the period of account determines the amount of writing-down allowances to which you are entitled.

Thus, if a period of account:

- is only nine months long, 9/12 of the writing-down allowances can be deducted from taxable profits for that period; or

- extends to 15 months, the tax deductible allowances equal 15/12 of the writing-down allowances.

Should a period of account exceed 18 months, it must be divided into one of 12 months and a balancing period with restricted writing-down allowances.

There is a section in the supplementary self-employment pages in which you must summarize your claim to capital allowances.

Losses

> ## Tax Saver
>
> It is almost inevitable that your business will go through both good and bad times. If so, you need to be aware of, and to consider, all of the different options for claiming the tax relief due on the loss.

If you incur a loss you can claim tax relief on the loss sustained as increased by the amount of your capital allowances for the same period. You can choose whether to set a trading loss against other income in either the same, or the preceding, tax year. But you cannot claim to relieve only part of a loss.

> Isabel Fletcher has been in business for many years. She makes up her accounts to 31 August each year. In the year ended 31 August 2021 she makes a loss that she can claim against her other income in 2021/22. Alternatively, the loss can be carried back and relieved against her total income in 2020/21.

Any unrelieved loss of your business then has to be carried forward for offset against profits from the same business in future years.

Alternatively you can claim to set a trading loss against capital gains (see Chapter 13) in the following way.

- The claim is for relief on the amount of the trading loss that cannot be set against your other income in the year or on which tax relief has already been given in some other way.

- The maximum loss eligible for relief against capital gains is the same as the amount of your gains chargeable to Capital Gains Tax.

It is not possible to make a partial claim.

Tax Saver

By relieving a business loss this way you may be wasting personal allowances as well as your annual exemption for Capital Gains.

Tax relief for losses incurred by new businesses is extended such that:

- losses incurred during the first four tax years can be set against your total income for the three years prior to that in which the loss arises; and

- relief is first of all given against total income for the earliest year. For example, if you set up in business during 2020/21 and sustained a loss in the first period of trading, that part of the loss attributable to the 2020/21 tax year can be set against your income in 2017/18, 2018/19 and 2019/20, beginning with 2017/18.

There is one final type of loss relief that is only available to those businesses that incur a loss in their last period of trading. In such circumstances there cannot be future profits against which such a loss might be relieved. Therefore, a loss arising in the last 12 months of trading can be set back against the profits from the same business in both the final and three preceding tax years, beginning with the profits of the last year and working backwards.

Ralph Collins retires from business on 30 September 2021. In the final nine months in business he loses £18,000. Previously his business had always been successful as follows:

Accounting year	Taxable profits (£)	Year of charge
Year ended 31 December 2017	16,000	2016/17
Year ended 31 December 2018	12,000	2017/18
Year ended 31 December 2019	9,000	2018/19
Year ended 31 December 2020	4,000	2019/20

The terminal loss can be set off as follows:

2020/21	£4,000	leaving nil taxable profits
2019/20	£9,000	leaving nil taxable profits
2018/19	£5,000	reducing the taxable profits to £7,000
	£18,000	

Limit of reliefs

There is a limit on the amount of certain Income Tax reliefs that you can claim. This annual 'cap' is the greater limit of:

- £50,000; or
- 25 per cent of your total income.

The reliefs caught by this rule include:

- claiming to set off early year, annual or post-cessation trading losses against other income, but not capital gains; and
- qualifying loan interest (see Chapter 4).

In 2021/22 Ben Turner suffered a loss of £60,000 in his business. Ben made a claim to offset this loss against his total income for the year of £140,000. The maximum loss that can be relieved is £50,000 as this is more than £35,000 (25 per cent of Ben's income of £140,000).

The restriction of relief for business losses may have a significant adverse impact on the finances of owners of any small- or medium-sized businesses:

- suffering a blip in profitability; or

- investing in plant or machinery to take advantage of the Annual Investment Limit.

Taking on staff

You have now reached the time where your business is expanding. You need an assistant or an extra pair of hands. When you start employing staff you need to register:

- as an employer with HMRC; and

- before the first payday.

I suggest you do this online.
As an employer, you are responsible for several things:

- Working out the deductions for Income Tax (PAYE) and National Insurance Contributions from the salary or wage paid to your employees at regular weekly or monthly intervals.

- Paying over the deductions to the Collector of Taxes each month. These payments can be made every quarter where your average monthly payments of PAYE and National Insurance Contributions are less than £1,500.

- Letting your tax office know every year how much each employee has earned together with the deductions made for both Income Tax and National Insurance Contributions. The deductions should reconcile to the total of the amounts paid over to the Collector of Taxes. You must also give details of any benefits paid or provided.

- Giving your employees certificates showing their earnings for the tax year, deductions for Income Tax and National Insurance Contributions and the value of any benefits provided.

Some other ways to save on tax

Tax Saver

Look into taking your spouse/partner into partnership where he or she helps you in the business and your annual profits are such that the top slice is taxable at the higher 40 per cent or additional 45 per cent rates. Between you it may be possible to make significant savings in your overall annual tax bill.

Tax Saver

If your business is growing and becoming ever more profitable you should seriously think about transferring it to a limited company with the following advantages.

- The rate of tax paid by a company on its profits is much lower than the corresponding Income Tax rates on personal income.
- The members' liability is limited to the amount paid for their shares and any loans to the company.
- Once formed a company can exist forever.
- No other person can use the company name.
- New shareholders and investors can easily be introduced.

Finally, when you want to retire it is far easier to:

- sell your stake in a company; or
- transfer ownership of your shares,

than sell, or pass on, a business operating as a sole trader.

Tax Saver

Finally, always look to the future and plan for your retirement, whether you are contemplating a sale of your business or handing it down to the next generation.

Foster carers

Those who receive income from local authorities or independent fostering providers for providing foster care to children and young people, or are qualified shared-lives carers are entitled to a special relief, which comes in two parts:

- an exemption from Income Tax on receipts that do not exceed the qualifying amount for any year; and

- a simplified optional method of calculating taxable profits where receipts are more than the qualifying amount.

The annual qualifying amount is made up of two parts, which must be added together. They are:

- a fixed amount for each household – £10,000 for 2021/22; and

- a weekly amount for each foster child placed with you – this varies by geography as well as age; see below for rates for 2021/22.

	Age 0 to 2	Age 3 to 4	Age 5 to 10	Age 11 to 15	Age 16 to 17
London	£155	£158	£177	£201	£235
South East	£149	£153	£169	£193	£226
Rest of England	£134	£138	£152	£173	£202

Where your receipts (fees, salaries, reward payments, allowances, etc) exceed the annual qualifying amount you can choose between paying tax on:

- your actual profits from foster caring, worked out on the principles that apply for any other business; or

- profits worked out on a simplified method, which is the difference between your total receipts for the year less the annual qualifying amount.

Whichever way you choose to be taxed you must at least keep records of your receipts and the ages and number of weeks that you care for each child placed with you. For this purpose a week runs from Monday to the following Sunday. Part of a week counts as a full week.

Furnished holiday accommodation

The letting of furnished holiday accommodation in both the United Kingdom and anywhere else in the European Economic Area may be treated as a trade as long as the property is:

- let commercially and furnished;
- available for letting commercially to the public as holiday accommodation for at least 210 days in a 12-month period; and
- actually let for at least 105 such days.

Any period exceeding 31 days during which the property is occupied by the same person does not count towards the 105 days test.

If, in any 12-month period, the periods of occupation of more than 31 days total more than 155 days the accommodation will not qualify under these rules.

Tax Saver

As the letting of furnished holiday accommodation is treated as a trading activity:

- you can claim capital allowances on expenditure for furniture and equipment in the holiday home;
- the profits count as earnings for pension purposes; and
- you can only claim relief for losses, including mortgage interest, against income from your furnished holiday-letting business.

Other special situations

So far, only a general picture of the way in which the profits of most businesses are taxed has been put forward. If you are a farmer, a writer, a Lloyds underwriter or a subcontractor in the construction industry, you should know that there are special rules for working out the taxable profits from these and some other trades, professions or vocations. In such situations it is advisable to seek professional assistance.

08
National Insurance and state benefits

Employed or self-employed, you must pay National Insurance Contributions as well as Income Tax on your earnings or business profits. By paying sufficient National Insurance Contributions you become eligible to claim those social security benefits that are based on your contribution history. Many benefits, mainly those payable to the disabled, do not depend upon the payment of contributions.

National Insurance numbers

You need to have a National Insurance number (NINO) so that all the contributions you make can be properly recorded. It is unique to you and made up of two letters and six numbers, followed by a further letter – A, B, C or D. You keep the same number for your whole life.

All children are notified of their NINO shortly before their 16th birthday providing:

- they live in the UK; and
- their parents or guardians are receiving Child Benefit for them.

Or else you can apply at any time over the age of 16:

- in order to claim tax credits and/or benefits;
- when you start in employment or working for yourself; or
- if you have applied for a student loan.

If any of these circumstances apply, and you are under 20 years old, you should contact the National Insurance Registrations Helpline on 0300 200 3500. Otherwise, you should call the National Insurance number application line on 0800 141 2075.

National Insurance Contributions

There are four classes of contribution payable as follows:

- Class 1 by employees;
- Class 2 by the self-employed;
- Class 3 which is voluntary; and
- Class 4 by the self-employed, based on profits of your business.

The rates of National Insurance Contributions for 2021/22 are listed in Appendix 3.

At the present time there is a gradual increase in State Pension Age for both men and women to:

- age 66; then
- to 67 and 68,

depending on when you were born.

You do not have to go on paying contributions once you attain State Pension age, even if you carry on working either:

- in employment; or
- for yourself in your own business.

On 27 October 2021, in the Autumn Budget a Health and Social Care Levy to fund social care reforms was revealed.

From April 2022, this applies to employees and employers liable for Class 1 NI contributions and self-employed individuals liable for Class 4 NI contributions.

The average basic-rate employee earning £20,000 per annum will contribute an additional £130 a year. Meanwhile a typical higher-rate employee earning £80,000 per annum will pay a further £880 a year.

It is important to note the NIC increase will also apply to employers too, who will pay an additional 1.25 per cent in employer NIC from April 2022.

Employers will have to pay the levy for employees earning above the Secondary Threshold of National Insurance, which is £8,840 in 2021–22. Existing reliefs will continue to apply for employers of apprentices under the age of 25, all employees under the age of 21, veterans, and new employees in freeports from April 2022.

(a) Class 1

The earnings of employees on which contributions are calculated include:

- a salary or wage – before deduction for pension contributions;
- overtime, bonuses and commission;
- holiday pay; and
- Statutory Sick, Maternity and Paternity Pay.

No contributions are payable by employees on:

- business expenses;
- tips and gratuities; or
- redundancy payments.

The contributions you pay are usually a percentage of your weekly or monthly salary or wage, subject to lower and upper-earnings limits that change from year to year. The rate and amount of contribution you pay when you return to work is unaffected if:

- you change jobs and have a break between them; or
- there is a period when you are unemployed.

Tax Saver

If you have more than one employment you must pay contributions on your earnings from all your jobs. However, there is an overall annual maximum limit of contributions payable by employees. You can apply for a refund in any year where the total contributions you have paid exceed this annual limit. Alternatively, by completing form CA72A, you can apply for deferment where you reckon that the contributions you will pay on earnings from two or more employments will exceed the maximum annual limit.

The National Insurance Contributions and Employer Office of HMRC will then instruct one or other of your employers not to withhold contributions from your earnings. After the end of the tax year your overall contribution history is reviewed. If you have not paid enough contributions the National Insurance Contributions Office will send you a calculation and a demand for the balance due.

(b) Class 2

This is a weekly flat rate payable by the self-employed. They are collected through the tax system with both Income Tax and Class 4 contributions.

If your business profits are less than a specified limit each year (£6,515 for 2021/22) you are exempted from paying contributions. But you should apply in advance for what is known as small-earnings exception.

(c) Class 3

The payment of these flat-rate contributions is voluntary. It may sometimes be beneficial to pay Class 3 contributions, such as when you have been:

- in a job but your wage was below the lower earnings limit;
- abroad; or
- in prison.

Ask HMRC to check your National Insurance Record. They will be able to tell you:

- if you can make these voluntary contributions; and
- how much you can pay.

By doing so you fill in gaps in your contribution history. This will help in satisfying the requirement for benefits such as the State Pension.

(d) Class 4

These are payable by the self-employed based on a percentage of taxable business profits, after capital allowances, but before relief for pension contributions. They are paid each year through self assessment along with the Income Tax due on business profits.

The profits of Jack Wagstaff's business, as adjusted for tax purposes, are £43,311 for 2021/22. For the same year his claim to capital allowances amounts to £7,954, giving a net chargeable amount of £35,357. He pays Class 4 National Insurance Contributions of £2320.92 as follows:

	£	£
On the first	£9,569	Nil
On the next	25,788 @ 9 per cent	2320.92
		2320.92

Tax Saver

You do not have to pay if you:

- are under 16 years old; or
- reach pension age before the start of the tax year.

Social Security benefits

Responsibility for administering all aspects of the Social Security system lies with the Department for Work and Pensions (DWP). There are local DWP offices all across the country. The framework of the Social Security system is now so substantial, and the range of benefits so wide and varied, that it is only possible for me to give a brief summary of the main state benefits that fall into these categories:

- working-age benefits (for those under pension age), administered by Jobcentre Plus;
- pension-age benefits (for those of pension age and over), administered by the Pension, Disability and Carers Service;
- tax credits (see Chapter 3) and Child Benefit for families with children and people in work, administered by HMRC; and
- disability and carer benefits, administered by the Department of Work and Pensions.

Many benefits are only payable to individuals with an established National Insurance Contribution history. The type of benefit you can claim depends on the class of contributions paid as follows:

Type of benefit	Class 1 (Employed)	Class 2 (Self-Employed)	Class 3 (Voluntary)
New State Pension	Yes	Yes	Yes
Bereavement Allowance	Yes	Yes	Yes
Bereavement Payment	Yes	Yes	Yes
Widowed Parent's Allowance	Yes	Yes	Yes
Jobseeker's Allowance	Yes	No	No

(continued)

(Continued)

Type of benefit	Class 1 (Employed)	Class 2 (Self-Employed)	Class 3 (Voluntary)
Employment and Support Allowance, contribution-based	Yes	Yes	No
Statutory Sick, Maternity and Paternity Pay	Yes	No	No
Shared Parental Pay	Yes	No	No
Maternity Allowance	Yes	Yes	No

Other benefits do not depend upon the payment of contributions.

(a) Statutory Sick Pay

To be able to claim Statutory Sick Pay you must be paying sufficient Class 1 contributions. Other main points are:

- it is a flat-rate cash payment made to employees by their employer;
- to claim you must be both incapable of work and not actually do any work at all on the day in question;
- it is not payable for the first three agreed qualifying days in any period when you are too unwell to work; and
- in any period of sickness you have a maximum entitlement to 28 weeks of Statutory Sick Pay.

(b) Statutory Maternity Pay

Eligibility for Statutory Maternity Pay is again dependent on the payment of Class 1 contributions. A woman:

- qualifies for Statutory Maternity Pay if she has been working continuously for the same employer for 26 weeks up to, and including, the 15th week before her baby is due;
- must provide evidence of being pregnant and give her employer sufficient notice of leaving work; and
- will receive benefit for 39 weeks beginning not earlier than the 11th week before the baby is due, although she can actually select the time over which she will be absent from work.

(c) Statutory Paternity Pay

The basic features of ordinary Statutory Paternity Pay are:

- fathers are allowed up to two weeks away from work during the first eight weeks of their child's life;
- it is also a flat-rate cash payment; and
- the qualifying requirements are the same as those for Statutory Maternity Pay.

(d) Shared Parental Leave and Pay

As the name implies, the purpose behind these benefits is to allow eligible couples to swap the role of the main carer of their child between them.

You can either:

- be having a baby; or
- adopting a child.

You can go to the GOV.UK website to find out:

- if you can get Maternity, Paternity or Shared Parental Leave; and
- how much you will receive if you take leave.

(e) Jobseeker's Allowance

The key points of the Jobseeker's Allowance, which is taxable, are:

- entitlement is based on either a satisfactory contribution record or a means-tested low income;
- it is payable to unemployed individuals between the ages of 18 and state pension age who are not in full-time education, are available for work and are actively seeking employment;
- it is a weekly benefit with supplements for age and other personal circumstances;
- an applicant is allocated a work coach to help in making a plan to find work which could involve taking part in a Work Programme; and
- payments will be suspended for a time if a claimant fails to keep to a Work Programme or does not carry out something requested by their work coach.

(f) Employment and Support Allowance

Employment and Support Allowance helps people with ill health or disability move into work.

You may be able to claim this allowance if you are:

- no longer receiving Statutory Sick Pay or Statutory Maternity Pay and have not returned to work;
- not getting Jobseeker's Allowance; and
- under State Pension age.

While your claim is being assessed you will have to:

- undertake a Work Capability Assessment; and
- complete a questionnaire about your ability to work.

You will then be allocated to either:

- the work-related activity group where you will have frequent interviews with an adviser; or
- the support group without interviews.

There are three types of Employment and Support Allowance:

- contribution-based;
- income-related; and
- 'new style'.

To be able to claim the contribution-based type:

- you must have paid enough National Insurance Contributions; and
- payment is limited to one year.

You may be able to claim the income-related kind:

- if you do not have enough money coming in; or
- if you have not paid enough National Insurance Contributions and you satisfy the entitlement conditions.

To be eligible for the 'new style' version you must already be receiving Universal Credit.

It works in the same way as the contribution-based type.

(g) Income Support

Income Support is a non-contributory weekly benefit paid to eligible individuals who do not have sufficient money to live on. You get:

- a basic payment depending on your status; and
- extra payments called premiums if:
  - your partner is a pensioner; or
  - you are disabled or a carer.

(h) Universal Credit

Universal Credit has now been introduced across the United Kingdom. It replaces many of the previous benefits and is exempt from tax.

Universal Credit has replaced the following means-tested benefits and tax credits:

- Income-based Jobseekers Allowance;
- Income-related Employment and Support Allowance;
- Child and Working Tax Credits;
- Income Support; and
- Housing Benefit.

You do not need to do anything about moving to Universal Credit until you hear from the DWP.

(i) Child Benefit

Child Benefit is payable:

- to individuals bringing up children;
- for all children under 16 years old; and
- for children over age 16, but under 19, providing they are still in full-time education, which includes courses at school or college up to A-level.

It is not means-tested and for couples who are married it is the mother who should make the claim.

High-income claimants receiving Child Benefit:

- are subject to a tax charge (see Chapter 11); but
- can opt not to receive the benefit if they or their spouse/partner want to avoid paying the charge.

> **Tax Saver**
>
> Electing not to receive Child Benefit, in order to avoid the High Income Child Benefit Charge (see Chapter 11), is not the same as not making a claim in the first instance. A claim should always be made and then followed by the opt out. This ensures the claimant, usually the mother, is credited with National Insurance Contributions. As a result entitlement to the State Pension or other benefits is not jeopardized.

(j) Personal Independence Payment

To be eligible for a Personal Independence Payment (PIP) you must:

- be aged 16 to 64;
- have a long-term health condition or disability; and
- have difficulties with daily living activities or mobility.

PIP:

- is tax-free; and
- comprises standard and enhanced components for both the daily living and mobility components.

Gradually PIP is replacing the Disability Living Allowance currently paid to claimants of that allowance.

(k) Attendance Allowance

Attendance Allowance is paid to people over the age of 65 who:

- are seriously disabled, mentally or physically; and
- need a lot of care and attention both throughout the day and at night.

Capital limits

If your capital is over £16,000, you will not be entitled to:

- Universal Credit;
- Income Support;

- Housing Benefit; or
- Income-related Jobseeker's Allowance and Employment and Support Allowance.

The amount of the above benefits you will receive is tapered where your capital is between £6,000 and £16,000. Capital includes:

- cash;
- funds held in a bank or building society account; and
- shares or investment trusts at market value or surrender rate less 10 per cent.

Cap on benefits

The maximum weekly amount that individuals can receive in benefits depends on where they live as follows:

Claimant	Inside Greater London (£)	Outside Greater London (£)
Single adults	296.35	257.69
Couples	442.31	384.62
Single parents whose children live with them	442.31	384.62

The 'cap' applies to the combined amounts of:

- Jobseeker's Allowance;
- Incapacity Benefit;
- Income Support;
- Employment and Support Allowance;
- Housing Benefit;
- Child Benefit;
- Child Tax Credit;
- Universal Credit; and
- Bereavement, Widowed Parents, Maternity and Severe Disablement Allowances.

Some households including those with someone receiving:

- Personal Independence Payment;
- Disability Living Allowance;
- Carer's or Guardian's Allowances;
- Attendance Allowance; or
- the Support component of the Employment and Support Allowance,

are exempt, as are war widows, widowers and households with someone entitled to the Working Tax Credit.

Benefits and rates

Listed in Appendix 4 are all the Social Security benefits, distinguishing between those that are taxable and non-taxable.

Following on is Appendix 5, which gives the rates of the main Social Security benefits for 2021/22.

State Pension Credit

An individual is entitled to the State Pension Credit if he or she:

- lives in Great Britain;
- satisfies at least one of two requirements of the guarantee and savings credits respectively; and
- has reached the qualifying age.

Tax Saver

The guarantee credit 'tops up' your weekly income to £177.10 per week if you're single for 2021/22, and to £270.30 jointly if you have a partner.

A claimant's income includes:

- a state and any other pension;
- earnings;
- some Social Security benefits; and
- notional investment income of £1 a week for every £500 of savings or capital in excess of £10,000 (excluding your home and possessions).

The purpose of the savings credit, the rules for which are far from simple, is to reduce Pension Credit by 40 per cent of the amount by which a pensioner's income exceeds the appropriate minimum guarantee.

The guarantee credit is available to:

- both men and women who have reached the State Pension age for women; and
- a member of a couple where the other partner has attained the State Pension age for women.

The qualifying age for both men and women increases to age 65 for the savings credit element.

09
State and private pensions

I don't doubt that when you give up work and retire you will want to be able to maintain your lifestyle and living standards. You may have built up savings while you were working, but your income in retirement is most likely to come from:

- the State Pension; and
- an employer or personal pension scheme.

So that you can give yourself the best possible opportunity to build up a good pension, you should start contributing to a plan as soon as you can reasonably afford to do so.

The new State Pension

If you attained the State Pension age after 5 April 2016 you are eligible for the new State Pension.

The full new State Pension is £179.60 per week. However:

- your National Insurance record is used to work out how much you will actually receive;
- you usually need at least 10 qualifying years before you are entitled to any new State Pension;
- to get the full new State Pension you must have 35 qualifying years; and
- you may be able to pay Voluntary National Insurance Contributions if you have gaps in your contribution history that would stop you getting the full pension.

You may get credits towards your National Insurance Contributions record if you:

- are a carer;
- unemployed; or
- cannot work because of a disability or illness.

You should receive a letter, about four months before you reach your State Pension age, telling you what to do and how to make your claim. You can do this:

- online;
- over the telephone; or
- by downloading the State Pension claim form.

If you are widowed you might be able to inherit an extra payment in addition to your new State Pension. But this will not apply if you:

- remarry; or
- form a civil partnership before you attain State Pension age.

Deferment

Until 5 April 2016 you could defer taking your State Pension and either:

- receive an increased pension when you actually take it; or
- be paid a lump sum.

If you opted for a simple addition to your future State Pension, the higher weekly payment you got is the amount that is taxable.
Under the lump sum alternative:

- the rate of pension was fixed at the time you applied for deferral;
- the single payment comprises both pension arrears, including increments, and interest thereon;
- the total amount is liable to Income Tax;
- it is not added to income for any tax purposes;
- it does not impact on the calculation of the amount of the age-related married couple's allowance;
- the tax you pay on the lump sum is worked out by applying your marginal rate of tax;

- the Pension Service will deduct tax at source based on your declaration indicating your likely band of taxable income;
- you can elect for it to be paid and, therefore, taxed in the following tax year;
- you can do this at any time from the date you choose to receive the lump sum up to one month later;
- no further interest is added to the lump sum;
- the minimum deferral period is one of 12 consecutive months; and
- there is no maximum length of time for which drawing your State Pension can be deferred.

But bear in mind that:

- if you die before you claim your State Pension; and
- have no surviving spouse or civil partner,

the lump sum is lost.

Archie Barber was entitled to draw his State Pension in June 2019 but decided against doing so at the time. He chose to take his lump sum, amounting to £18,500, three years later in June 2022. In 2021/22 his total income, all from pensions, amounted to £29,000. He pays tax of £3,700 on his lump sum as follows:

	£
Pensions	29,000
Less: Personal allowance	12,570
Taxable income	16,430
2021/22 tax due: £16,430 × 20 per cent	3,286
Tax payable on lump sum State Pension: £18,500 × 20 per cent (as a 20 per cent taxpayer)	3,700

If you put off claiming the new State Pension:

- there is no lump sum payment; and
- you only get an increased regular pension.

State Pension forecast

As you approach retirement age, for State Pension purposes it is a good idea to get a forecast of what you will receive from the DWP.

You can get a State Pension forecast if you are more than 30 days away from State Pension age when your application is processed. Your forecast will advise you in today's money of:

- how much State Pension you may get; and
- the number of qualifying years on your National Insurance record.

The application form BR19 is available from the Pension Service by telephoning 0800 731 0175. Alternatively, the forecast can be obtained online.

Private pensions

There are a number of attractions in saving for your retirement through a private pension plan. If you are self-employed you will need to make your own arrangements. For those of you working in employment your employer will be running a scheme for the employees of the business that you can join.

Tax Saver

The main features of pension provision are:

- you receive full tax relief on your allowable premiums;
- your contributions are invested in a tax-free fund;
- you can take your benefits from the age of 55; and
- you do not have to retire to access your benefits.

(a) Annual contributions

You can get tax relief on the payment of pension contributions:

- up to 100 per cent of your annual earnings; but
- subject to a maximum annual allowance, which is £40,000.

However the allowance is:

- reduced by £1 for every £2 of your net income above £240,000; but
- reduced to £4,000 when your income is £312,000 or more.

Furthermore, once you start drawing taxable income from your pension fund you are also restricted to paying pension contributions not exceeding £4,000 each year.

The annual allowance:

- does not set a limit on pension contributions in a tax year; but
- is by reference to the 'pension input period' for each pension scheme ending in a tax year.

In calculating how much has been contributed you need to take into account:

- payments into all your pension schemes ending in the tax year; and
- any employer contributions.

If more than the annual allowance is contributed, the excess is taxed at your marginal rate of tax.

(b) Unused allowances

If your contributions exceed the annual allowance in a tax year, you will not be liable to the excess charge providing you have sufficient unused allowances brought forward from the three previous years.

Contributions are first of all allocated to the annual allowance for the current year. Any excess can then be set against any unused allowances brought forward. Those of an earlier year are used first.

Warren Baker is employed as a senior manager on a salary of £50,000 per annum. He is a member of his employer's pension scheme, which has a pension input period running from each 1 April to the following 31 March. The company contributes 10 per cent of Warren's salary towards his pension. He pays in 6 per cent of his salary. The contributions each year from Warren and his employer total £8,000.

In June 2022 Warren is awarded a bonus of £100,000 by his employer for securing a valuable long-term contract for the company.

Warren decides to pay £80,000 from the bonus into his pension as a one-off extra contribution. Warren's pension input amount in 2022/23 of £88,000 (£80,000 + £8,000) exceeds his annual allowance by £48,000. However, he has unused annual allowances brought forward from previous years as follows:

	Unused allowances brought forward (£)	Utilized in 2022/23 (£)	Carried forward (£)
2021/22	32,000	–	32,000
2020/21	32,000	16,000	16,000
2019/20	32,000	32,000	–
		48,000	

First of all Warren uses up his unused allowance from 2019/20. This is followed by £16,000 from 2020/21 leaving unused allowances from 2020/21 and 2021/22 totalling £48,000 to carry forward to 2023/24.

(c) Drawing your pension from age 55

Tax Saver

Until you dip into your pension fund it is called an uncrystallized fund. Twenty-five per cent of any lump sums taken out of the fund are tax-free; the balance is taxed as income.

But once you start taking a regular income by:

- going into a regular drawdown plan; or
- purchasing an annuity,

only the first withdrawal of 25 per cent, or less, of the full value is free of tax.

However tempting it may be to withdraw a large chunk of money in one tax year from your pension savings, you need to be aware that you could incur a very substantial tax bill.

In 2021/22 John Hill has earnings of £25,000. His tax bill, all at 20 per cent, is £2,500. His pension pot is £200,000 and he decides to take half of it. 25 per cent of the £100,000 withdrawal is tax-free leaving £75,000 taxable. His tax liability for 2020/21 increases to £27,539 as follows:

	£
Taxable pension fund withdrawal	75,000
Earnings	25,000
	100,000
Less: Personal allowance	12,570
Taxable income	87,430
Income Tax payable	
£37,159 @ 20 per cent	7,431
£50,271 @ 40 per cent	20,108
	27,539

Just over 66 per cent of the taxable part of the withdrawal bears tax at 40 per cent. If John had encashed the entire fund:

- the tax-free amount increases to £50,000, but
- he would have lost his personal allowance of £12,570; and
- some of the pension pot would suffer tax at 45 per cent.

Tax at source under the PAYE system is taken off by your pension provider on both:

- lump sum payments; and
- regular income,

drawn from your pension pot.

As it is more than likely that too much tax will be deducted from lump sum withdrawals, the following forms are available from HMRC to reclaim any tax overpayment. These are:

- Form P50Z, which is used if you have cashed in your entire pension fund and you have no other income in the year;

- Form P53, which is relevant if you have withdrawn all your pension pot but you do have other taxable income in the year; and

- Form P55, which applies when you make a partial withdrawal but no further cash withdrawals are intended in the same tax year.

Savers who are thinking about taking money from their pension funds can access free guidance so they can better understand their retirement income options under these rules. This is available from either:

- Pension Wise, a free service set up by the Government; or

- Citizens Advice.

(d) Small pension pots

If the amount of your pension savings is:

- less than £30,000 you can take it all in cash; or

- no more than £10,000 in each of three pension pots you can do the same.

However, remember that only 25 per cent of any lump sum is tax-free.

(e) Lifetime allowance

There is a single lifetime allowance of £1,073,100 on the amount of your pension savings you can build up during your life that can benefit from tax relief. If the value of your pension fund is more than the lifetime allowance when you come to draw your pension you will be subject to tax on the excess, as follows:

- at 55 per cent if paid as a lump sum; or

- at 25 per cent on a taxable pension.

(f) Fixed protection

There are two ways you can protect pension rights built up from the lifetime allowance tax charge.

This is another aspect of your tax and financial affairs on which you should seek specialist advice.

(g) Death benefits

On death, special rules apply to funds held in a pension pot because Inheritance Tax (see Chapter 17) is not usually charged on money held in a pension.

Tax Saver

If you die before age 75 and leave funds in a defined contribution pension fund your nominated beneficiaries can inherit the fund tax-free. This applies whether they:

- take one or more lump sum withdrawals; or
- use the fund for income.

But if you are over 75 years old when you die, a beneficiary who opts for:

- a lump sum; or
- regular amounts,

will pay Income Tax at his or her marginal rate on what they receive.

Kevin Arnold and his wife, Stella, have two children, Evan and Ella. Kevin has a defined contribution pension fund amounting to £560,000. He nominates Stella as the beneficiary of the fund in the event of his death. Kevin dies at age 74. Stella opts not to encash the fund tax-free. Instead she withdraws a regular income which is not taxable.

Stella then nominates her two children as equal beneficiaries of the remaining fund. Stella dies at age 78. As she is over age 75 on her death, Evan and Ella will pay Income Tax at their respective marginal rates on whatever they withdraw from the fund.

Stakeholder pensions

Tax Saver

Even if you are not:

- earning; or
- paying tax,

you can contribute up to £3,600 per annum into a pension scheme and obtain tax relief at the basic rate.

You can set up a scheme for your spouse and each child or grandchild. As much as £2,880 can be invested every year into each separate pension plan. The remaining £720 is contributed by HMRC.

10
Savings and investment income

There are likely to be occasions during your lifetime when you will either be:

- making regular savings out of income;
- investing a lump sum from a pension scheme on retirement; or
- in receipt of a much more substantial sum such as an inheritance or, perhaps, winnings on the National Lottery.

Examples of savings and investment income are:

- bank or building society interest;
- share and unit trust dividends;
- rents;
- interest on government stocks; and
- income from a trust fund.

Tax-free income

Tax Saver

The most widely known investments where the return is tax-free are some of those available from National Savings and Investments. Individuals in the top tax brackets should take a look at them. They are:

- Fixed-Interest and Index-Linked Savings Certificates*; and
- Premium Bond Prizes.

*Although no issues are on general sale at the time of writing, the total value of any maturing certificates can be renewed.

Since 1 May 2019 National Savings & Investments (NS&I) have changing the inflation measure they use to calculate returns on their index-linked savings certificates from the Retail Price Index (RPI) to the Consumer Price Index (CPI).

Also tax-free are:

- interest on cash ISAs;
- dividends from ISA investments; and
- dividends paid on shares in Venture Capital Trusts.

Tax-free income does not need to be reported on your annual Income Tax Return.

Savings income

Savings income is that such as interest on:

- your bank/building society accounts;
- holdings of British Government stocks;
- National Savings Guaranteed Growth and Income Bonds, Savings and Investment accounts; and
- any other interest-bearing accounts or funds.

You will:

- receive your interest without any deduction for tax; and
- may also get up to £1,000 of tax-free interest depending on which tax bracket you are in.

Known as the Personal Savings Allowance, the amounts of tax-free savings income for 2021/22 are as follows:

Type of taxpayer	Amount of tax-free savings income (£)
Basic rate	1,000
Higher rate	500
Additional rate	Nil

Furthermore, a zero rate applies to the first £5,000 of taxable savings income. But this zero rate is only available on any part of your taxable savings income:

- of up to £5,000; and
- after taking off your personal allowance.

Tax Saver

To get all the interest on your savings income tax-free in 2021/22, your taxable income for the year should usually not exceed £18,570, comprising:

- your personal allowance of £12,570;
- the Personal Savings Allowance of £1,000;
- plus £5,000.

But it can be more if you are entitled to other allowances, such as:

- the relief given to a registered blind person;
- the married couple's allowance; and
- the new transferable marriage tax allowance.

However, because earnings and pensions are treated as the first slice of taxable income, many taxpayers will not benefit from this nil tax rate on the first £5,000 of taxable savings income.

Florence Kirk earned £15,850 and had savings income of £3,000 during 2021/22. She paid Income Tax of £856, calculated as follows:

	£	£
Total income		18,850
Less:		
Personal allowance	12,570	
Personal Savings Allowance	1,000	
		13,570
Taxable income		5,280

(continued)

(*Continued*)

	£	£
Income Tax payable		
£1,000 @ 0 per cent		Nil
£4,280 @ 20 per cent		856
		856

Florence's personal allowance of £12,570 is first of all set against her earnings of £15,850, which restricts the amount of her savings income taxable at 0 per cent by £3,350.

Dividend income

For 2021/22:

- the nil rate band on dividend income remains at £2,000; and
- the rates of tax payable on dividends above the allowance stay as follows:

For dividends otherwise taxable at	Rate (%)
Basic rate	7.5
Higher rate	32.5
Additional rate	38.1

All of the rates will rise by 1.25 per cent from April 2022. In working out how much tax you pay each year, dividend income is always regarded as the top part of your income. Following an announcement in the Autumn Budget 2021, from the 2022–23 tax year, basic rate dividend tax will be charged at 8.75 per cent instead of 7.5 per cent for 2021/22. Higher rate dividend taxpayers will be charged at 33.75 per cent instead of 32.5 per cent and additional rate dividend taxpayers will pay 39.35 per cent instead of 38.1 per cent respectively.

Tanya Bridge earns £10,850 and receives dividends of £8,000 in 2021/22. She pays tax of £375 for the year as follows:

	Income source (£)	Personal allowance (£)	Basic rate band (£)
Earnings	10,850	10,850	–
Dividends	8,000	1,000	7,000
Totals	18,850	11,850	7,000
Less: Dividend allowance			2,000
Taxable income			5,000
Tax payable @ 7.5 per cent			375

This calculation will change from April 2022.

Tanya's sister, Henrietta, is retired. In 2021/22 she receives £22,500 from pensions and £25,000 from dividends. She pays tax of £3,850 for the year as follows:

	Income source (£)	Personal allowance (£)	Basic rate band (£)	Higher rate band (£)
Pensions	22,500	12,570	9,930	–
Dividends	25,000	–	24,500	500
Totals	47,500	12,570	34,430	500
On dividends			24,500	500
Less: Dividend allowance			2,000	–
			22,500	500
Tax payable @ 7.5 per cent/ 32.5 per cent			1,687.50	162.50

In addition Henrietta pays tax of £2,000 on her pensions.

This calculation will change from April 2022.

Accrued income

Interest on fixed-rate investments is regarded as accruing from day-to-day between payment dates. On a sale the vendor is charged Income Tax on the interest that has accrued from the previous payment date to the date of sale. The purchaser is allowed to deduct this amount from the interest received on the following payment date.

These arrangements cover both fixed and variable-rate stocks and bonds, including those issued by governments, companies and local authorities. But the arrangements will not affect you if the nominal value of your securities is under £5,000.

The interest on a holding of 6 per cent Treasury Stock 2028 is payable on each 7 June and 7 December. The half-yearly interest on a holding of £30,000, sold for settlement on 15 August 2018, is £900.

$$\text{Accrued proportion} = \frac{69 \times £900}{183} = £339.34$$

Rents

The letting of property, including isolated or casual lettings, is treated as a business for tax purposes. This applies to any flat, house, shop or other property that you rent to tenants. Most of the rules for working out the taxable profits from a trade or profession are also relevant in working out your annual income from the letting of property. It follows, therefore, that if you are eligible you may want to adopt the cash accounting rules for businesses (see Chapter 7) in working out the taxable profit from your property letting activity.

Income from all your properties in the United Kingdom is pooled together, regardless of the type of lease. Also it does not matter whether the property is let furnished or unfurnished.

However, unlike a trade or profession, losses from your property rental business can only be carried forward to be set against future profits from the same activities.

Other than expenditure of a capital nature, such as that on extensions, structural alterations or improvements, the general running costs of a property can be set against rental income. Included in allowable expenses are:

- fees incurred on letting out the property, including estate agents' costs and those for drawing up the tenancy agreement and an inventory;
- rent collection and management costs;
- interest relating to your property letting business (see Chapter 4);

- replacing or repairing any items such as a sink, boiler, radiator, bath, shower which are fixed to the property;
- replacing loose domestic items like carpets, curtains or other soft furnishings;
- general maintenance and redecorations;
- insurance premiums on buildings and contents policies;
- ground rent for leased premises;
- water rates and Council Tax;
- gardening, cleaning and security services;
- all other expenses of managing the property such as stationery, postage, advertising for tenants, etc; and
- your share of expenditure on the common parts of the let property.

As an alternative to claiming:

- capital allowances; and
- actual expenses, such as fuel

you can opt for a fixed-rate deduction (see Chapter 7) for every mile you travel by car, motorcycle or goods vehicle on your property letting business. There is a tax-free allowance of £1,000 for individuals such as:

- Airbnb hosts; and
- those whose income from letting property is small.

The rules are the same as those which govern the small business income allowance.

Karen Donnelly owns a flat that she let out to tenants during 2021/22. The net rental income for the year amounts to £14,090 as follows:

	£	£
Rent receivable from the flat		21,000
Less: Expenses		
Agents fees for letting	2,467	
Management fees	740	
Ground rent	200	
Service charges	1,103	
Council tax for tenants	960	

	£	£
Water rates	220	
Replacing bedroom curtains	650	
Lounge redecoration	490	
Boiler repair	80	
		6,910
2021/22 net rental income		14,090

Rent-a-room

Income from the furnished letting of spare rooms in your home as residential accommodation is tax-free providing the gross rents do not exceed £7,500 per annum. The space you let out must be in your only or main home, which can be a house, flat, caravan or even a houseboat.

Where your annual gross rents are more than £7,500 you must elect if you want to pay tax on the excess gross rents, without any relief for expenses. If you do not do so then you will have to work out your taxable income using the rules for lettings income.

Theresa Stevens is a basic-rate taxpayer who lets out spare rooms in her bungalow to lodgers paying £160 per week between them, £8,320 for 2021/22. The expenses that could be set against the lodgers' rents total £1,800 for the year.

Theresa elects for rent-a-room relief and her Income Tax liability is £164.00 (£8,320 – £7,500) x 20 per cent. Under the normal rules her tax liability would come to £1,304.00 (£8,320 – £1,800) x 20 per cent.

The tax-free limit of £7,500 is halved where an individual and some other person are each entitled to income under the scheme. Each lessor's exempt amount is then £3,750.

Tax Saver

You can elect to opt out of this special form of relief. It will benefit you to make the opt-out election if, for example, there is a loss on the letting that can be set against your other rental profits under the normal rules dealing with income from lettings.

Tax Saver

If you need more income and do not want to move home, why not rent out a room to a lodger or bed-and-breakfast guest? Up to £7,500 a year (equivalent to a weekly rent of £144.20) is tax-free under this type of relief.

Non-qualifying life policies

At the outset, a lump sum premium is paid into a bond that is, for example, either investment based or intended to produce a guaranteed income. An investor can usually:

- take regular amounts out;
- make ad hoc partial withdrawals; or
- leave the bond untouched until encashment or death, when it will form part of the investor's estate.

There is no tax relief on the single premium. Neither Capital Gains Tax nor Income Tax at the savings rate is payable on any profit. But investors whose income takes them into either the higher or additional rates of 40 per cent or 45 per cent will pay tax at the difference between their top rate and the basic rate of Income Tax on chargeable events. These arise on:

- surrender or maturity of the policy;
- death of the life assured; or
- withdrawals in excess of a cumulative allowance built up at the time.

At the end of each policy year an allowance of 5 per cent of the original investment is given. This can be carried forward from year to year. Over a period of

20 years, allowances of up to 100 per cent of the initial investment will be given. A taxable gain only arises if the amount of the withdrawal is more than the cumulative allowance at the time. Then it is the excess that is taxed.

Edward Clark invests £15,000 in an investment bond. Withdrawals of £600, £900 and £3,250 are made during the second, third and fifth policy years. The annual allowance is £750, being 5 per cent, of the original investment. A taxable gain of £1,000 arises in year five as follows:

Number of policy years	Cumulative allowance (£)	Amount withdrawn (£)	Cumulative withdrawal (£)	Taxable amount (£)
1	750	–	–	–
2	1,500	600	600	–
3	2,250	900	1,500	–
4	3,000	–	1,500	–
5	3,750	3,250	4,750	1,000

In some cases, a wholly disproportionate liability to tax can arise on a part surrender. In such cases taxpayers can ask HMRC to recalculate historic charges on a just and reasonable basis.

When the final chargeable event on a bond occurs, the taxable gain is calculated by taking into account all previous withdrawals and taxable gains.

After seven years, Edward encashes the investment bond in the illustration above for £21,050. The taxable gain amounts to £9,800 as follows:

	£	£
Policy proceeds		21,050
Add: Withdrawals in years 2, 3 and 5		4,750
		25,800
Less:		
Original investment	15,000	
Amount already taxed	1,000	
		16,000
Taxable gain on encashment		9,800

The method of calculating the Income Tax due on the taxable gain involves a number of stages, including 'top slicing' relief.

Edward is a single man. During 2021/22 his other income, all earnings, amounted to £45,850. He pays tax of £1,259.30 on the gain of £9,800 on the final encashment of his bond worked out as follows:

Gain on encashment of bond	£9,800
Number of years held	7
Taxable slice of gain	£1,400
Taxable income – excluding slice of gain	
Earnings	£45,850
Less: Personal allowance	£12,570
	£33,280
Tax applicable to slice of gain	
On first £500 (£34,500 – £34,000) @ 0 per cent	–
On next £900 (excess over £34,500) @ 20 per cent (40 per cent – 20 per cent)	£180.00
Average rate on slice	12.85%
The tax payable on the gain = £9,800 @ 12.85 per cent	£1,259.30

Tax Saver

A non-qualifying life policy such as a single premium investment bond is a good way to supplement your income, particularly for anyone in the top tax brackets.

Individual Savings Account

An Individual Savings Account (ISA) can include:

- cash (including National Savings); or
- stocks and shares.

> **Tax Saver**
>
> You do not pay any tax on the interest you earn in a cash ISA. Also free of tax are the income or capital profits in a stocks and shares ISA.

You can subscribe to an ISA if you are:

- both resident and ordinarily resident in the United Kingdom for tax purposes; and
- aged 18 or over, although 16- and 17-year-olds can invest just in cash.

> **Tax Saver**
>
> The annual subscription limit for all qualifying individuals:
>
> - is £20,000 in cash;
> - can be saved in just one type of account or split between both kinds; and
> - is increased each year in line with the Retail Prices Index rounded to a convenient multiple of £120 to allow for the easy calculation of monthly contributions.

> In May 2021 Lance Bishop put cash of £9,000 into a stocks and shares ISA. This left him with up to £11,000 available to invest in either a cash ISA or his stocks and shares ISA during the rest of 2021/22.

You can make withdrawals and then replace money in your cash ISA within the same tax year without these transactions counting towards your annual subscription limit.

Tax Saver

Spouses and civil partners can make an additional contribution to their ISAs equivalent to the value of their deceased spouses' or partners' ISAs at the date of death. You are allowed:

- three years after the death of your spouse or civil partner; or
- 180 days after the administration of the estate is complete, if later,

in which to make this contribution which could result in significant savings in tax for the future.

Other features of an ISA are:

- there is no statutory lock-in period or minimum subscription;
- you can make withdrawals whenever you like; and
- there is no lifetime investment limit.

The list of investments that qualify for the stocks and shares component include:

- shares listed on a recognized Stock Exchange;
- shares quoted on the Alternative Investment Market;
- Unit Trusts;
- Investment Trusts;
- open-ended investment companies (OEIC); and
- government stocks with at least five years to go to maturity.

Lifetime ISA

Taxpayers can also take out a Lifetime ISA into which:

- they can save up to £4,000 each year until age 50; and
- the government will make an additional 25 per cent contribution to the savings in the account.

The funds in this new ISA must either:

- be used to assist with the purchase of a first home costing up to £450,000; or
- withdrawn tax-free after an individual reaches age 60.

Failing this, the government bonus, plus any interest or growth in the account, must be repaid. A 5 per cent levy will also be charged.

Monies saved through a Lifetime ISA count towards the annual ISA subscription limit.

Help-to-Buy ISA

This tax-free savings scheme closed to new accounts on 30 November 2019. It was available to anyone aged 16 or over saving for a deposit on their first home. If you have already opened a Help-to-Buy ISA (prior to 30 November 3019), you are able to continue saving into the account until November 2029. There are two important key features of these accounts for first-time buyers:

- They are limited to one for each individual, rather than one per home – so those buying together were able to open an account each.
- You were able to save up to £1,200 in the first month. In each subsequent month this limit is £200. But you cannot save through both Help-to-Buy and cash ISAs in the same tax year.

Tax Saver

The government contributes 25 per cent tax-free to your savings at the time you use it for a deposit on your first home. You need to save at least £1,600 to qualify for the minimum bonus. The maximum bonus is £3,000 on savings of £12,000.

The bonus is only paid when you buy your first home in the UK. It is only available on purchases of up to £250,000 outside London and £450,000 in London.

Should you subsequently decide not to buy a house the account will still be tax-free. However, you will not qualify for the government bonus.

Help-to-Save

Launched in September 2018, the Help-to-Save Scheme, a government-backed secure savings account, is:

- targeted at those on low incomes; and
- to help them boost their savings.

You can open a Help-to-Save account if you are either;

- entitled to Working Tax Credit; or
- claiming Universal Credit.

You:

- can contribute up to £50 each calendar month over four years;
- do not have to save every month;
- get a tax-free bonus of 50p for every £1 you save. Bonuses are paid at the end of the second and fourth years based on the amount of your savings; and
- can close your account whenever you want. But you may miss the next bonus and you cannot open another account.

After four years your account:

- will be closed; and
- you can retain all the funds in it.

Enterprise Investment Scheme

The aims of the scheme are twofold:

- to provide a targeted incentive for equity investment in unquoted trading companies, which helps overcome the problems faced by such companies in raising modest amounts of equity finance; and
- to encourage outside investors previously unconnected with the company, who introduce finance and expertise, by allowing them actively to participate in the management of the company as paid directors without losing entitlement to relief.

There are several features of EIS.

- Income Tax relief at 30 per cent on qualifying investments up to £1 million in a tax year.

- Subject to the annual £1 million subscription limit, the Income Tax relief can be carried back to the previous year.

- All shares in a qualifying company must be held for at least three years, otherwise the Income Tax relief will be clawed back.

- Losses made on the disposal of qualifying shares are eligible for relief from either Income Tax or Capital Gains Tax.

Seed Enterprise Investment Scheme

This scheme:

- runs alongside the Enterprise Investment Scheme; but

- is targeted at smaller companies in the early stage of their development.

There are several features of Seed EIS.

- Income Tax Relief at 50 per cent on qualifying investments up to £100,000 in a tax year.

- The 50 per cent rate of relief does not depend on the investor's top personal tax rate; it is calculated on the amount invested and given as a credit against the investor's total tax liability.

- The Income Tax relief can be carried back to the previous year.

- All shares in a qualifying company must be held for at least three years, otherwise the Income Tax relief will be clawed back.

Venture Capital Trusts

Venture Capital Trusts (VCTs) are a type of Investment Trust with tax advantages designed to encourage investment in the under-nourished small business sector. Individuals investing in VCTs are eligible for the following Income Tax incentives.

- Relief at 30 per cent on subscriptions for new ordinary shares up to £200,000 in any tax year, providing the shares are held for at least five years.

- Tax-free dividends.

The 30 per cent Income Tax relief is deductible from the total Income Tax payable and does not depend on the investing individual's marginal tax rate.

Overseas investment income

Generally, income from investments or savings abroad is taxed in the same way as your onshore dividends or interest income. Foreign tax paid, subject to certain restrictions, can be offset against the tax payable here on the same income. If required, you must be able to show that you have actually paid, or suffered, the overseas tax.

Joint income

Income from assets such as bank/building society accounts, property or shares held in the joint names of a married couple or civil partners is treated for tax purposes as belonging to them in equal proportions. If the actual proportions of ownership between the couple are unequal, they can make an election for the income on any jointly owned assets to be taxed in accordance with their respective entitlements to the income. There is a special form to complete. The declaration applies from the date it is made.

But dividends from jointly owned shares in a small family company are taxed on each spouse or civil partner according to their actual ownership, rather than in equal shares.

Tax Saver

Income splitting is likely to be of relevance to some taxpayers as a means of reducing their overall tax burden in view of:

- the restriction to the personal allowance for individuals with incomes of more than £100,000; and
- the 45 per cent rate of Income Tax on incomes in excess of £150,000.

11
The family unit

Gone are the days when it was commonplace for couples to marry. Many now prefer to live together as partners. Couples may have children without marrying, or marry later on in life.

Living together

There are no special tax breaks for couples living with one another as partners. They are each taxed as single people. Furthermore, it is mandatory that income from jointly owned assets must be split between them in accordance with the ratio of their respective interests in such assets. Assets cannot be transferred between them without avoiding a possible liability to Capital Gains Tax at the time of transfer.

Marriage/civil partnership

Spouses or civil partners:

- are taxed separately on their income and capital gains;
- are each entitled to personal allowances that can be set against their own income, whether from earnings or investments;
- can each have taxable income, after allowances and reliefs of £37,700 for 2021/22 before either of them is liable to tax at the higher rate of 40 per cent (they may, of course, need to rearrange their affairs to take maximum advantage of potential tax savings; in contrast to the position of unmarried couples this is easily done);
- must complete their own Tax Returns every year; and
- are each responsible for settling their respective tax liabilities.

Children

A child or teenager is:

- treated as an individual for tax purposes like anyone else;
- entitled to the personal allowance – £12,570 for 2021/22 – so no tax is payable on any earnings or other income up to this limit; and
- a taxable person for the purposes of Capital Gains Tax (Chapter 13) and Inheritance Tax (Chapter 17).

But, the income from a gift by a parent in favour of an unmarried minor child is regarded as the parents' income for tax purposes – subject to an annual £100 limit for small amounts of income.

Tax Saver

Grandparents or other relatives can, however:

- give savings to their grandchildren, nieces, nephews, etc, without the same restrictions applying to the taxation of income on any such gifts; or
- with the benefit of professional advice, set up a discretionary settlement with grandchildren among the class of beneficiaries. Such trusts suffer tax at 45 per cent on their income. As a result, taking the personal allowance into account, all or some of the tax suffered by the trustees on the income paid out for the benefit of a minor beneficiary should be repayable.

A few years ago Jeremy Chandler created a discretionary trust. In 2021/22 the trustees resolved to distribute income of £2,000 for the benefit of his young granddaughter, Veronica. This is her only income in the year. Her parents can recover Income Tax of £1,636 for Veronica as follows:

	Income (£)	Tax (£)
Trust distribution	3,636	1,636
Less: Personal allowance	12,570	
Taxable income	Nil	
Repayment for 2020/21		1,636

Parents, civil partners or those responsible for children do not get a general tax allowance for their children. However, there are other ways to claim benefits of tax credits if you are responsible for children:

- You should be able to claim Child Benefit. It does not depend on income.
- If you are on a low or modest income, you should be able to claim the Child Tax Credit.
- Depending on your personal circumstances you may be entitled to one or more of the numerous other Social Security benefits associated with children.

It is down to parents or guardians to complete and sign Tax Returns or Repayment Claims for their children up to age 18.

High Income Child Benefit Charge

This is a charge on a taxpayer:

- who has net income of more than £50,000 in a tax year; and
- either they, or their partner, is receiving Child Benefit.

Where both spouses or partners have net incomes exceeding £50,000, the charge is paid by the spouse or partner with the higher income.
The tax liability:

- is charged at 1 per cent for each £100 of net income between £50,000 and £60,000; and
- is equal to the amount of Child Benefit where net income exceeds £60,000.

Claimants of Child Benefit can opt not to receive the benefit if they or their spouse/partner want to avoid paying the charge.

Joel Haynes and his wife, Cleo, have two children. Joel's adjusted net income for 2021/22 is £58,500. Cleo received Child Benefit totalling £1,820 for the year (£21.05 each week for the elder child plus £13.95 a week for the younger child = £35 × 52 weeks = £1,820.00). Joel's High Income Child Benefit Charge for 2020/21 is £1,547 = 85% (£58,500 − £50,000 ÷ 100) × £1,820.00.

Tax-Free Childcare

This scheme is available for working families, whether:

- employed;
- self-employed; or
- on parental, sick or annual leave,

to help with the cost of childcare.

To qualify, parents:

- must be in work; and
- earn at least the National Minimum Wage or Living Wage for working 16 hours a week. This works out at £142.56 for anyone aged 23 or over but is due to rise to £9.50 an hour from April 2022; but
- not more than £100,000 a year.

For every 80p contributed by eligible families the government will put in 20p, thereby providing support of up to £2,000 a year for each child. This limit doubles for a child with a disability.

The scheme is available for children under:

- the age of 12; or
- the age of 18 for those with disabilities.

Adopted children are eligible but foster children are not.

The scheme:

- operates through an online Childcare account with National Savings and Investments in conjunction with HMRC;
- replaces the Childcare Voucher Scheme.

The Child Trust Fund

The main features of Child Trust Funds (CTFs) still in existence are:

- Up to £9,000 in total can be added to the fund each year by family and friends.
- All income and capital growth within a CTF is tax-free.
- It can be accessed at age 18.

There are a wide range of organizations offering CTF accounts linked to either cash deposits, unit trusts or even equities.

It is now possible for parents with CTFs to get a better deal by transferring the funds to Junior Individual Savings Accounts.

Junior Individual Savings Account

Any child resident in the United Kingdom, under the age of 18, and who does not have a Child Trust Fund account, is eligible for a Junior Individual Savings Account (JISA).

Tax Saver

A JISA is a tax-efficient way to save for your child's future. There are several key features of a JISA savers should be aware of.

- The account can be opened and managed by the person with parental responsibility for the child.
- Up to a fixed amount can be invested each year.
- The annual investment limit for 2021/22 is £9,000.
- All returns are tax-free.

Other features of a JISA are:

- family or friends can also contribute up to the amount of the annual allowance;
- the funds in a JISA can be invested in cash or stocks and shares; and
- it can be accessed by the child at age 18.

Separation and divorce

Not only does the breakdown of a marriage cause much personal suffering but it invariably has consequences for tax purposes.

A married couple are no longer considered to be living together when:

- they are separated by a Deed or Court Order; or

- they are living apart in such a way that permanent separation is inevitable.

If a married couple are entitled to the married couple's allowance, the full allowance can be claimed by the husband or wife for the tax year in which the marriage fails. However, if he or she remarries in the same year he or she cannot also claim that part of the allowance due for the period following the wedding.

Maintenance payments are tax-free in the hands of the recipient, but only limited tax relief is available to the payer of maintenance under a Court Order, Child Support Agency assessment or written agreement as follows.

- Either the payer or recipient must be born before 6 April 1935.

- The payment must be to the divorced or separated spouse.

- The maximum amount of tax relief to which the payer is entitled in 2021/22 is 10 per cent of the lesser of £3,530 or the actual maintenance paid each year.

- No tax relief can be claimed on maintenance paid to, or for the benefit of, children of the marriage.

The tax implications for civil partners who separate are no different to those for a married couple. Similarly the dissolution of a civil partnership has the same consequences as a divorce.

Old age

When it comes to tax, getting older does not mean an easier life. Pensioners have to deal with the tax system in the same way as everyone else. Nevertheless, there are some factors that are only relevant to:

- the finances of elderly persons; and

- working out how much tax they must pay each year.

First and foremost comes the married couple's allowance. In Chapter 2, I explained how an older taxpayer calculates the amount of this allowance to which he or she is entitled. Of particular significance:

- are the rules allowing elderly couples to transfer the married couple's allowance between them, which can sometimes save on tax; and

- is the income limit for the married couple's allowance, which is by reference to the husband's income or that of the spouse/civil partner with a higher income as the case may be. These rules apply even if entitlement to this allowance arises because of the age of the other spouse/civil partner.

On reaching State Pension retirement age (see Chapter 8) you have three options:

- retire and claim the State Pension;
- carry on working and claim the State Pension; or
- put off claiming the State Pension.

All pensions, including a State Pension, are taxable. There is, however, no mechanism to deduct any Income Tax at source from payment of the State Pension. Therefore, in addition to including a pensioner's personal allowance in the coding notice of an occupational or personal pension taxed under PAYE, a deduction from allowances equivalent to the annual amount of the State Pension is also incorporated.

If a pensioner's State Pension and other deductions exceeds his or her personal allowance, HMRC issue a 'K' Coding. The amount of the negative allowance is then added to the pension on which tax is paid.

Taxpayers approaching State Pension age should make sure that their Notice of Coding is changed to include an estimate of the amount of their State Pension for the year. Usually HMRC sends such taxpayers a Form P161 asking for details about pension entitlement. This information is then used to amend tax codes as appropriate.

Nowadays many people carry on working after they retire from their main job or self-employment. They may decide to make use of all the knowledge and experience built up during their working lives by setting up in business as a consultant, or take a part-time position in, for example, a retail outlet.

Owen Wilcox is single and age 69. During 2021/22 he received a State Pension of £137.60 per week and an annual pension from his previous employer of £8,000. To keep himself occupied he worked part time at his local DIY store, earning a weekly wage of £105 for 46 weeks of the year. Owen paid Income Tax for 2021/22 of £1,483 as follows:

	Income (£)	Tax (£)
State Pension	7,155	–
Occupational pension	8,000	540
Wages	4,830	966
	19,985	
Less: Personal allowance	12,570	
Taxable income	7,415	
Income Tax payable		
£7,311 @ 20 per cent		1,483

The tax code used for working out the Income Tax to be deducted from Owen's occupational pension is 552L. This is based on the difference between Owen's personal allowance of £12,570 and his State Pension of £7,155. Tax at the basic rate of 20 per cent, under a BR Code, would have been deducted from Owen's wage from the DIY store.

Tax Saver

Elderly couples, in particular, need to pay great care and attention to their respective incomes. They should make sure that their investments and savings are arranged such that they:

- do not lose out on the married couple's allowance, only for taxpayers born before 6 April 1935; and

- take maximum advantage, if possible, of the generous annual amount that can be invested in ISAs.

They should also remain mindful of the annual income limit above which this allowance is restricted. As a result it may benefit couples to transfer capital between them.

Death

Sadly, death comes to all of us and has tax consequences for married couples, which are as follows.

- The married couple's allowance is not restricted in the year of death of either spouse.
- Where the husband dies first, he is due his full personal allowance in the year of death. If he cannot use up the full married couple's allowance, because he has a low income, then the balance can be transferred to his widow.
- If the wife dies before her husband, she will be due her full personal allowance in the year of death.

Civil partners are treated no differently.

12
Residence and domicile

As a general rule Income Tax is charged by the United Kingdom on:

- an individual's income arising in the United Kingdom irrespective of whether that person is resident here; and
- overseas income belonging to an individual resident in the United Kingdom.

Apart from some special cases, the amount of tax you pay each year depends on:

- whether you are resident in the United Kingdom; and
- in some circumstances on your domicile.

Not only are the two concepts of residence and domicile of fundamental importance in working out an individual's liability to UK taxation on income, but they are equally relevant for the purposes of both Capital Gains Tax and Inheritance Tax.

Residence

There are statutory rules to determine whether an individual is, or is not, a resident in the UK. Under the statutory residence test, an individual is tax resident if either of the following are met, namely:

- automatic residence test; or
- the sufficient ties test which determines residence status based on a combination of days spent in, and various ties with, the UK.

The automatic residence test

If you can answer 'yes' to any one of the following overseas tests you are automatically not resident in the UK for that tax year.

• Did you spend less than 16 days in the UK?*

• Were you in the UK for less than 46 days and have you been not resident in the UK for all of the previous three tax years?

• Were you in full-time employment abroad and spent less than

    o 91 days in the UK; and

    o fewer than 31 of those days working in the UK?**

However, you are automatically UK resident for a tax year if you:

• are not automatically non-resident; and

• can reply 'yes' to any of these UK tests.

They are:

• Did you spend more than 182 days in the UK?

• Did you work full-time in the UK?

• Did you have a UK home in which you resided for more than 30 days, with no home abroad?***

*This test does not apply if you die in the tax year. It is then replaced by other tests.
**A day at work in the UK means that you spend at least three hours working in the UK on that day.
***A home in the UK is any property which is available to you for at least 91 days in the tax year.

Sufficient ties test

This is an alternative test if you do not meet either the automatic overseas or UK residence tests.

Then, the UK residence for a tax year of either:

• an individual leaving the UK to go abroad (a 'leaver'); or

• a person coming to the UK from overseas (an 'arriver'),

depends on:

• how many days they spend in the UK; and

• how many of the following five connecting factors that they satisfy.

These are as follows:

- Is your family UK resident?
- Do you have accommodation in the UK which is available to you?
- Have you spent at least 40 days working in the UK?
- Have you been in the UK for more than 90 days during either of the last two tax years?
- Have you spent more time in the UK than in any other country? ('leavers' only).

If you are:

- a 'leaver'; and
- have been UK resident in any one of the last three tax years,

your residence status is determined by the following table.

Days spent in the UK	Only resident if you satisfy
Less than 16	Always non-resident
16 to 45	Four or more connecting factors
46 to 90	Three or more connecting factors
91 to 120	Two or more connecting factors
121 to 182	One or more connecting factors
Over 182	Always resident

If you are:

- an 'arriver'; and
- have not been UK resident in any one of the last three tax years,

your residence status is governed by the following table.

Days spent in the UK	Only resident if you satisfy
Less than 16	Always non-resident
16 to 45	Always non-resident
46 to 90	Four or more connecting factors
91 to 120	Three or more connecting factors
121 to 182	Two or more connecting factors
Over 182	Always resident

Working abroad: expenses

Tax relief is allowed on the costs you incur on travel expenses in relation to your overseas employment. Nor will you be taxed on the following expenses borne by your employer.

- The cost of board and lodging outside the United Kingdom.
- Your travelling expenses, which also extends to unlimited return visits to the United Kingdom during longer assignments abroad.
- The travelling expenses of your spouse, civil partner or children to visit you overseas. No more than two return visits by the same person are allowed each year and you must be working abroad for a continuous period of at least 60 days.

Leaving the United Kingdom permanently

Where you go abroad to live permanently, or are outside the United Kingdom for three years or more, you will cease to be UK resident from the day following your departure.

Before you leave, ask your tax office for the special form (P85) relevant to individuals going abroad. You can use this form to claim tax relief or a tax refund for the year during which you leave the UK if you:

- worked or lived here;
- are leaving;
- may not come back; or
- are going to work abroad full time for at least one full tax year.

The information on the form will also enable HMRC to consider your residence position.

As a non-resident, you will not usually pay UK tax on:

- the State Pension; and
- interest on government securities.

Allowances for non-UK residents

If you are not resident here but have taxable income in the United Kingdom, you may be able to reduce your tax bill by claiming UK tax allowances.

These will generally be the same as those granted to an individual resident in the United Kingdom and can be claimed by the following individuals:

- a national of a state within the European Economic Area;
- a present or former employee of the British Crown;
- a resident of the Isle of Man or the Channel Islands;
- a widow or widower of a Crown Servant;
- a person employed by a missionary society; or
- a person abroad for health reasons following UK residence.

Tax Saver

To claim:

- the allowances to which you are entitled; and
- any resulting tax repayment,

you will need to complete form R43 available from HMRC.

Other non-resident individuals may be able to claim UK tax allowances under the Double Taxation Agreement concluded between the country where they are resident and the United Kingdom.

Income from UK property

Many individuals rent out their homes while they are living or working overseas. You can apply to HMRC for a certificate authorizing your tenant, or managing agent, to make payments of rent to you without withholding any UK tax. If you do not apply for a certificate or one is not issued to you, tax at the basic rate must be withheld from all remittances of rent to you by your managing agent or tenant.

Whether or not tax is deducted by your tenant or letting agent, while you are non-UK resident you are still liable to UK tax on income arising from the letting out of your property here.

However, you will not have to pay any UK tax if your income from property after allowable expenses, and any other taxable income, is less than any UK tax allowances that you may be entitled to claim.

Tax Saver

Non-resident married couples or civil partners with let property in the United Kingdom should consider putting their properties into joint ownership. It might then be possible for both parties to claim their personal allowance in working out the tax payable on their respective shares of the rental income.

Double taxation relief

If you move to a country with which the United Kingdom has concluded a Double Taxation Agreement, you may be able to claim partial or full exemption from UK tax on certain types of income such as:

- pensions and annuities; and
- royalties and dividends.

Furthermore, many Double Taxation Agreements contain clauses dealing with the special circumstances of:

- teachers and researchers;
- students and apprentices; and
- entertainers and sports people.

Going abroad: Capital Gains Tax

If:

- you have been resident in the United Kingdom for at least four out of the last seven years ending with the day before you leave; and
- within five complete years, you return here to take up residence for tax purposes again,

you will remain within the charge to Capital Gains Tax.
It follows that:

- gains realized in the tax year of departure will be taxed in that year; and
- all gains in subsequent years, including the year of return, will be subject to tax in the year when residence resumes.

However, profits made on assets bought and sold during the years of non-UK tax residence are tax-free in the United Kingdom.

Albert Rogers, who had lived his whole life in the United Kingdom, accepted an offer to work abroad and left the United Kingdom on 27 March 2018. On 17 July 2019 he sold an investment, which he owned when he left the United Kingdom, realizing a profit of £25,000. He returned to the United Kingdom to take up residence again on 3 November 2019.

As Albert:

- had only been abroad for three complete tax years (2018/19, 2019/20 and 2020/21); and

- was a resident in the United Kingdom for at least four of the seven tax years preceding his departure,

he will have to pay Capital Gains Tax on the gain of £25,000 in 2021/22.

Residential property in the United Kingdom

If:

- you are non-resident; and
- have sold or disposed of UK residential property,

you must tell HMRC within 30 days of conveyance.

You have to report the disposal within this time limit even if:

- the disposal results in a loss;
- there is no tax to pay; or
- you are already registered for Self Assessment.

Only that part of the gain relating to the period after 5 April 2015 is taxable. There are two ways of working this out. Either by:

- establishing the value of the property on 5 April 2015 and then calculating the gain based on this amount; or

- apportioning the gain equally over the total period of ownership.

The following chapter on capital gains sets out:

- the various reliefs; and
- the rates of tax,

for working out how much tax will be payable on the profit you made.

Coming to the United Kingdom permanently

Perhaps:

- you have been working overseas, your contract has finished and you have decided to return home; or
- you lived abroad and have now accepted a job offer in the United Kingdom.

You should:

- let HMRC know when you arrive in the United Kingdom; and
- apply for a National Insurance number (NINO) if you do not already have one and intend to work here.

You can claim the full UK personal allowance for the year of arrival. Where your job is with either a UK or an overseas employer and the duties of that employment will be performed wholly in the United Kingdom, the full amount of your salary will be taxable here.

Tax Saver

Before you leave the country where you have been living there may be opportunities to save on UK tax before taking up residence here. For example, it may pay you to close any bank or building society accounts before arrival as you would otherwise face the prospect of a charge to UK Income Tax on interest accrued, but not credited, while abroad.

Domicile

Domicile:

- is a concept of general law; and
- is distinct from residence or nationality.

When you are born you acquire a domicile of origin from your father. Until you are 16 years old your domicile follows that of the person on whom you are legally dependent. At age 16 you have the option to abandon your existing domicile in favour of a domicile of choice. To do so you must sever all links and leave your current country or state and settle elsewhere. You will need to provide good evidence of your intention to live there indefinitely or permanently.

A wife's domicile is not necessarily the same as her husband's if they were married after the end of 1973. It is governed by the same factors as for any other individual with an independent domicile. However, a woman who married before the beginning of 1974 automatically acquired her husband's domicile on marriage. As long as the marriage lasts, her domicile only alters when there is any change in the domicile of her husband.

Taxation of non-domiciliaries

Adult non-UK domiciled taxpayers who are claiming to be taxed on remittances of income to the United Kingdom, and who claim non-UK domiciled status when claiming the remittance basis on their annual Self Assessment Tax Return:

- will lose their entitlement to the personal allowance on income and the annual exempt limit on capital gains; and
- will have to pay an annual charge in order to claim the remittance basis unless unremitted foreign income and gains are less than a de minimis limit of £2,000.

The annual charge:

- is £30,000 for an individual who has been resident for at least 7 of the previous 9 tax years;
- increases to £60,000 for an individual who has been resident for at least 12 of the previous 14 tax years;

- is payable in addition to Income Tax due on income remitted to the United Kingdom; and

- is not itself taxed as a remittance if paid directly from an offshore source to HMRC.

Furthermore, the unremitted income or gains on which the tax charge is paid will not be taxed again if and when remitted to the United Kingdom.

Tax Saver

A non-domiciled taxpayer can, however, bring overseas income and gains into the United Kingdom free of tax for the purposes of making a commercial investment in a qualifying business.

Taxpayers who can claim the remittance basis do not have to do so. If they do not:

- they will then be taxed in the same way as other UK residents on income and gains arising in the tax year;

- tax will be payable on their worldwide income and gains for that tax year;

- they will be able to claim a personal allowance and the annual exempt limit on capital gains; and

- they will need to complete a Self Assessment Tax Return in order to report any foreign income and gains for that tax year.

Tax Saver

Individuals entitled to claim the remittance basis can decide from year to year whether they want to do so. In one year individuals:

- might choose to pay the annual £30,000 or £60,000 charge and lose their allowances; and

- in the next year opt to pay tax on their worldwide income and gains on the arising basis.

Non-domiciliaries:

- who have been resident in the UK for 15 out of the last 20 tax years will be deemed to have a UK domicile for the purposes of Income Tax and Capital Gains Tax. After a short period of grace comprising UK residence in at least one of the two previous years, their worldwide assets will also come within the scope of Inheritance Tax.
- born with a UK domicile, but who have subsequently acquired a domicile of choice in another country, are to be treated as domiciled here if they are resident in the UK.

As a consequence, individuals to whom these rules apply will be taxed on their worldwide income and capital gains as they arise.

I certainly recommend you seek professional advice on all of the taxation issues affecting non-domiciliaries as they are highly complex.

13
Capital gains

The profits you make on disposing of your assets are known as capital gains and are subject to Capital Gains Tax. However, not all capital receipts are taxable. These include:

- lottery, pools or gambling winnings;
- mortgage cash-backs; and
- personal or professional damages.

Profits made on disposing of the following assets are also tax-free:

- private cars;
- National Savings;
- your home;
- chattels sold for less than £6,000;
- British government securities and many corporate bonds;
- shares issued under either the Enterprise Investment or Seed Enterprise Investment Schemes as long as the Income Tax relief has not been withdrawn;
- shares in Venture Capital Trusts;
- shares issued under an employee shareholder agreement;
- investments in an Individual Savings Account (ISA);
- gifts to charities or for the public benefit; and
- qualifying life policies on your life.

Taxable gains

This list includes profits you realize from disposing of:

- property;
- shares and unit trust investments; or
- chattels sold for more than £6,000.

For Capital Gains Tax purposes, the date when the contract for purchase or sale is made determines the date when an asset is acquired or sold.

Tax payable

Every tax year you can make gains up to the annual exemption limit without paying tax. For 2021/22 the tax-free allowance is £12,300. Chargeable gains over and above this limit are taxed at different flat rates depending on both:

- the type of asset sold; and
- your income.

Band of taxable income (£)	Residential property* (rate of tax %)	Other assets (rate of tax %)
0–37,700	18	10
Above 37,700	28	20

*That which does not qualify for private residence relief; for example, buy-to-let.

Where your gains when added to your income exceed the basic rate limit of £37,699 for 2021/22 you will pay tax at:

- 10/18 per cent on the amount of the gains within the basic rate band; and
- 20/28 per cent on the excess.

Tax Saver

If, in the same tax year, you realize profits from selling both a buy-to-let and shares you can set your tax-free allowance against the gains taxed at the highest rate.

In 2021/22 Alastair McLaren made gains of £27,000 and £8,300 from selling an investment property and shares respectively. He pays tax at the higher rate. His Capital Gains Tax bill for the year is £5,864 as follows:

	£
Investment property gain	27,000
Less: tax-free allowance	12,300
	14,700
Profit on selling shares	8,300
	£23,000
Tax payable	
£14,700 @ 28 per cent	4,116
£8,300 @ 20 per cent	1,660
	£5,776

Tax Saver

Wherever possible try to utilize your full Capital Gains Tax Allowance limit each year. Any unused part of the annual limit is lost. It cannot be carried forward to future years.

Tax Saver

By realizing gains just after the end of a tax year you will delay payment of the tax for 12 months.

Tax Saver

By splitting sales across the end of a tax year you can make use of your annual tax-free allowance for two years.

Married couples/civil partners

Each spouse/civil partner is:

- separately entitled to the annual tax-free allowance limit; and
- individually taxed on chargeable gains they realize in a tax year in excess of the annual exemption limit.

A married couple living together can transfer assets between them without gain or loss as follows.

- The recipient spouse is deemed to have acquired such assets at the cost to the former spouse.
- This tax-free allowance ceases when a couple permanently separate.

It is not uncommon for a married couple to own assets in their joint names. For tax purposes, a profit on disposal of a jointly owned asset is apportioned between each spouse/civil partner in the ratio of their respective interests in that asset at the date of disposal.

Tax Saver

A husband and wife, or a couple in a civil partnership, each have their own annual exemption limit. They should consider transferring assets between them in order to use up both exemption limits.

Tax Saver

But this does not apply to married couples or civil partners who separate. The opportunity to transfer assets between them free of Capital Gains Tax terminates at the end of the tax year in which separation takes place. The moral here is to separate early on in a tax year to allow sufficient time to divide up valuable assets such as land and shares.

Working out chargeable gains

In calculating the taxable gain on the disposal of a chargeable asset, you are allowed to make certain deductions from the proceeds of sale as follows:

- the purchase price;
- incidental costs incurred on acquiring the asset;
- any additional expenditure you have incurred on enhancing the value of the asset, such as improvements or alterations to a property during your period of ownership; and
- the costs of sale.

The list of incidental expenses that are allowed as either purchase or sale costs includes:

- solicitor's fees, including transfer and conveyancing costs;
- surveyor's, valuer's or auctioneer's fees;
- broker's commission;
- estate agent's commission, including advertising expenses;
- Stamp Duty Land Tax; and
- valuation costs.

Relief for losses

Losses and gains made in the same tax year are offset against each other. Any excess losses can be carried forward, without time limit, to reduce gains in subsequent tax years. But losses can never reduce the amount of your gains to below the annual exemption limit.

Bernard Levy had unused capital losses of £9,700 at 5 April 2021. During 2021/22 he made gains of £23,700 and incurred losses of £8,500. His capital gains position for the year is:

	£	£
Gains realized in the year		23,700
Less: Losses		
in the year	8,500	
brought forward (part)	3,800	
		12,300
2021/22 Exemption limit		12,300

The unused losses at 5 April 2022 of £5,900 (£9,700-£3,800) can be carried forward to be set against gains in later years.

A loss:

- Arising on the sale or gift of an asset to a person with whom you are connected can only be set off against a gain on a similar disposal at a later date.

- Can be claimed where the value of an asset you own becomes negligible or nil. You do not actually have to dispose of the asset. The loss arises on the date that the relief is claimed. In practice, however, a two-year period is allowed from the end of the tax year in which the asset became of negligible value. In some cases the loss can be offset against income, giving you a bigger tax refund.

- On shares you subscribe for in a trading company not quoted on a recognized stock exchange can be set against your income, rather than against other capital gains. This applies whether you realize a loss on disposing of such shares or they become worthless.

Business Asset Disposal Relief

Business Asset Disposal Relief is a relief that can be claimed by individuals in working out their capital gains on the disposal of:

- all or part of a trading business carried on alone or in partnership;
- assets owned by an individual and used in his or her business;
- shares in an individual's own trading company; and
- shares in a trading company where an individual is an employee or officer of the company and:
  - owns at least 5 per cent of the company; or
  - has 5 per cent or more of the voting rights; and
  - from 29 October 2018 is entitled to at least 5 per cent of the distributable profits and net assets of the company.

The business, assets or shares, as the case may be, must be owned by the individual for at least a year prior to the date of disposal. However, on cessation a three-year time limit is allowed in which to make the disposal providing the individual satisfied the one-year requirement up to cessation.

Under Business Asset Disposal Relief the rate of Capital Gains Tax payable is 10 per cent on qualifying lifetime gains up to £1 million.

Gains made on disposals before 6 April 2008 do not count towards the lifetime allowance.

Tax Saver

It may pay you to look into how the ownership of your business is structured so that not only you, but also other family members, may be entitled to Business Asset Disposal Relief in working out the Capital Gains Tax payable on the profit on a future sale or disposal of the business.

In November 2021 Martin Osborne sold the shares he owned in his own trading company for £460,000. He originally bought the company in 1995 for £190,000. This was his only disposal in 2021/22. Martin pays Capital Gains Tax for the year of £25,800 as follows:

	£
Proceeds of sale	460,000
Less: Purchase price	190,000
Gain qualifying for Business Asset Disposal Relief	270,000
Less: Annual exemption limit	12,000
Gain chargeable to tax	258,000
2021/22 Capital Gains Tax @ 10 per cent	25,800

Investors' Relief

This is a relief on the disposal by investors of new ordinary shares in un-listed trading companies:

- subscribed for and fully paid in cash; and
- held for at least three years, starting from 6 April 2016.

There is no requirement for an investor to:

- be an officer or employee of the company; or
- hold more than 5 per cent of the shares or voting rights in it.

The rate of Capital Gains Tax payable is 10 per cent on qualifying lifetime gains up to £10 million.

Assets owned on 31 March 1982

Gains and losses on disposals of assets that you held on 31 March 1982 must be calculated solely by reference to their market value at that date, ignoring original costs.

Ashley Barker acquired a freehold factory in the late 1970s for £25,000. It was valued at £30,000 on 31 March 1982. Ashley sold the factory in May 2021 for £120,000, after expenses of sale.

The chargeable gain is £90,000 as follows:

	£
Sale price	120,000
Less: March 1982 value	30,000
2021/22 chargeable gain	90,000

Investments in shares

Before 6 April 1982, each shareholding was considered as a single asset and known as a 'pool' of shares. Every purchase of the same class of shares, or a sale of the part of the holding, represented either an addition to, or a disposal out of, the 'pool'. This changed when the indexation allowance was introduced. From 6 April 1982, each shareholding acquired was considered to be a separate asset. A further purchase of shares of a holding owned by you at 5 April 1982 could not be added to the 'pool'.

The rules were amended from 6 April 1985. Shares of the same class were again treated as a single asset growing or diminishing on each acquisition or disposal. This form of 'pooling' applied to shares acquired after 5 April 1982 unless they had already been disposed of before 6 April 1985. It was called a 'new holding'.

A 'pool' that was frozen under the 1982 rules had to stay that way. It continued as a single asset that could not grow by subsequent acquisitions and was known as a '1982 holding'. A '1982 holding' was treated like any other asset in working out entitlement to the indexation allowance. This was not so for a 'new holding'. It had to be continuously indexed each time there was an addition to, or a disposal out of, the 'pool' up until April 1998. All forms of 'pooling' ceased for shares acquired on or after 6 April 1998. This was when indexation was discontinued and replaced by taper relief. From that date until 5 April 2008 it was necessary to record and retain the date of acquisition of each holding of shares.

During this 10-year period the procedure for matching shares sold with their corresponding acquisition was as follows:

- shares acquired on the same day;
- shares acquired within 30 days following a disposal;

- shares acquired before the disposal, but after 5 April 1998, identifying the most recent acquisitions first;
- shares comprised in a 'new holding', the 1982–98 share pool;
- shares within a '1982 holding', the 1965–82 share pool;
- any shares acquired before 6 April 1965, last in first out; or
- shares acquired more than 30 days after the disposal.

Beginning with the 2008/09 tax year:

- following the withdrawal of both indexation and taper relief; and
- having to use the 31 March 1982 value, without exception, in working out capital gains and losses on disposals of assets acquired before that date, a simplified set of identification rules were introduced.

In the following order for shares of the same class that you own, these are:

- shares acquired on the same day;
- shares acquired within 30 days following a disposal; and
- shares in 'a pool', no matter when they were acquired, that grows or diminishes whenever any shares are acquired or disposed of.

Laurence Stone made the following purchases in the shares of a quoted company:

Date	No of shares	Cost
1 June 1978	3,000	£4,500
1 November 1987	3,500	£7,000
1 November 1994	1,500	£5,000
15 August 2021	4,000	£12,000

During 2021/22 he also made the following sales:

Date	No of shares	Sale proceeds
5 September 2021	2,000	£6,600
7 February 2022	6,000	£21,600

The shares were valued at £1.75 on 31 March 1982.

The 2,000 shares sold on 5 September 2021 must, first of all, be identified with part of the acquisition of 4,000 shares on 15 August 2021 as follows:

	£
Proceeds of sale	6,600
Less: Cost of 2,000 shares on 15 August 2021	6,000
Chargeable gain	600

The sale of 6,000 shares on 7 February 2022 must be matched with the same number of shares in 'the pool' as follows:

	No of shares	Cost/valuation (£)
Shares acquired on 1 June 1978 (at 31 March 1982 valuation)	3,000	5,250
Purchase in November 1987	3,500	7,000
Additional acquisition 1 September 1994	1,500	5,000
Purchase on 15 August 2021 (remainder)	2,000	6,000
	10,000	23,250
Proceeds of sale of 6,000 shares on 7 February 2022		21,600
Less: Deductible cost/value 6,000/10,000 × £23,250		13,950
Chargeable gain		7,650

The 'pool' of the remaining 4,000 shares, with a deductible cost/valuation of £9,300, is carried forward to future years.

The total chargeable gain on Laurence's two sales in 2021/22 is £8,250.

Whenever you receive a free or bonus issue of shares of the same class as an existing holding, the date of their acquisition is the same as that of the original holding. The same principle applies to further shares acquired under a rights issue.

Where a company in which you have a holding is taken over and you receive shares in the new company in exchange for your shares in the company taken over, no disposal for tax purposes takes place at that time. Your new holding is regarded as having been acquired at the same time, and for the same price, as the old one. If, however, you receive a mixture of cash and shares in the new company, a gain or a loss arises on the cash element of the takeover. It is then necessary to apportion the cost price of the old shares between the cash received and the value of the shareholding in the new company at the time.

Your home

The profit on the sale of your home is free of tax. The exemption automatically covers:

- the house; and
- the garden or grounds up to half a hectare, including the land on which the house is built.

A larger area of land can qualify for exemption where it can be shown that it was required for the enjoyment of the house.

For the exemption to apply in full you must live in your house throughout:

- the full period of ownership; or
- if later, since 31 March 1982.

However, where your home was bought before it had been built or completed:

- the ownership requirement will be met; but
- the occupation condition will not have been satisfied.

This is of particular relevance when it comes to purchases off-plan.

Where your home fails to meet all the exemption requirements, a proportion of the gain on sale is taxable. Certain periods of absence are, however, disregarded in determining whether the gain is totally tax-free.

Tax Saver

These are:

- the last 18 months of ownership always; and
- generally when you have to live away from home because of your work.

But this period extends to one of 36 months if:

- you are disabled; or
- move into long-term residential care.

Guy Robinson sold his home in February 2022, making a profit of £90,000 as worked out for Capital Gains Tax purposes. He had bought the property in November 2013.

His job had taken him abroad between March 2015 and May 2017. Shortly after his return he bought a new home and moved there in August 2017.

The time spent working abroad and the last 18 months from August 2019 are also considered periods when the property was Guy's main residence. The chargeable gain is, therefore, restricted to the part of the gain apportioned to the two years between August 2017 and August 2019 as follows:

$$\frac{\text{Chargeable period}}{\text{Period of ownership}} = \frac{24 \text{ months}}{87 \text{ months}} \times £90,00 = £24,827$$

Where part of your home is used exclusively for business purposes, such as a surgery or office, the proportion of the profit on sale attributable to the business use:

- is a chargeable gain; and
- qualifies for Business Asset Disposal Relief.

Tax Saver

If, during your period of ownership, a property is partly lived in as your home and rented out for the remainder of the time, the gain attributable to the period of letting that is exempt is the lower of:

- either £40,000; or
- an amount equivalent to the gain on the part you have occupied as your home.

Harriet Underwood made a taxable profit of £85,000 when she sold her flat in May 2021. She had acquired the property in April 2014 but only lived there from April 2018 until it was sold. For the remainder of the time the property was rented out. The chargeable gain is £11,000 as follows:

	£	£
Capital gain (period of ownership)		85,000
Less: Main residence exemption – 37 months	37,000	
Letting exemption – 48 months (lower of £40,000 or £37,000)	37,000	
		74,000
Chargeable gain		11,000

A second home

It is not uncommon these days for individuals to have two properties. The main home is usually a house or flat within a commutable distance from the office or other place of work. The second property might be in the country, by the seaside or abroad in a warmer climate.

Tax Saver

It is only the profit on the sale of your main residence that is free of tax. Which one of your two or more homes is considered your main residence is usually a matter of fact. It is, however, possible for you to determine this in writing to your tax office. In the election, you should state which of your homes you want regarded as your principal private residence for Capital Gains Tax purposes. The election can:

● commence from the date when you first have at least two homes available to you;

● apply from any time in the two years starting with the commencement date;

- be made retrospectively on any date within two years of the commencement date; or
- be varied as and when it suits you.

But you can only nominate an overseas property if you lived in it for at least 90 days in the tax year.

Spouses/civil partners are only allowed one qualifying home between them.

Tax Saver

However, spouses/civil partners should certainly consider owning a second home jointly. This could help reduce the Capital Gains Tax payable on a future sale as they may both be able to take advantage of their respective annual exemption limits in working out the tax payable on a profit on sale.

Pradeep and Sonia Singh bought their first home in January 2016 for £120,000. Not long afterwards Sonia received an inheritance from her father's estate and, with some of the money, they decided to buy a small flat by the seaside. This cost them £70,000 in October 2016. They elected for their first home to be their principal private residence for Capital Gains Tax purposes. In March 2022 they sold their holiday flat for £150,000, realizing a profit of £80,000. In order to reduce their tax bill, they changed their main residence election to the holiday flat for the final four weeks up to the date of sale. The taxable gain, split equally between them, is £52,830 as follows:

		£
Profit on sale		80,000
Less: Main residence relief (last 18 months)	$\left(\dfrac{18 \text{ months}}{53 \text{ months}}\right) \times £80,000$	27,170
Chargeable gain		52,830

Tax Saver

It is not uncommon for unmarried couples to each own a home. They may each be able to nominate a main residence for the purposes of Capital Gains Tax.

Tax Saver

If you own a home that was occupied rent-free by a dependent relative, then the profit on sale attributable to both their periods of occupation:

- up to 5 April 1988; and
- thereafter,

is tax-free.

Chattels

Profits from selling chattels with an expected life of more than 50 years that are sold for less than £6,000 are tax-free. Chattels include paintings and other works of art, antiques, furniture, jewellery, stamps and ornaments. Articles comprising a set are considered as a single item when they are sold to the same person but at different times.

For items that fetch between £6,000 and £15,000, the chargeable gain is restricted to 5/3 times the amount by which the proceeds of sale (ignoring expenses) exceeds £6,000 where this is to your advantage.

Meryl Nichols sold an antique vase at auction in March 2022 for £10,500, receiving £9,750 after expenses of sale. She had inherited the vase from her mother when she died in April 1987. It was then valued at only £1,000.

The chargeable gain is £7,500 as follows:

	£
Net sale price	9,750
Less: Acquisition cost	1,000
Profit	8,750
But restricted to 5/3 × £4,500 (£10,500 − £6,000)	7,500

When an article is sold for under £6,000 and at a loss, the allowable loss is restricted by assuming the sale proceeds were equal to £6,000.

> Vincent Wells bought a set of stamps in the late 1980s for £8,300. The set was sold in December 2021 for £6,600. Vincent's allowable loss is £1,700. If he had only made £3,800 on the sale, the tax loss would have been £2,300 (£8,300 – £6,000).

Gifts and valuations

There are times when a figure different from the actual disposal proceeds is used in the calculation of a capital gain. This happens, for example, when you make a gift or sell an asset at a nominal value to a close member of your family. On these occasions, you must work out the capital gain based on the open-market value of the asset at the time of gift or disposal.

There is a free service from HMRC that will help you whenever you need to use valuations to work out a gain or loss.

After you have made a disposal but before you make your return:

- you need to ask for one copy of Form CG34 for each valuation you want checked and confirmed; and

- you must then return the completed form to your tax office at least two months before the filing date for the Tax Return together with all the other information and documents requested on the form.

Agreed valuations will not subsequently be challenged when you submit your Tax Return unless you did not previously mention important facts affecting the valuations. If your figures are not agreed, HMRC will put forward alternative valuations.

> **Tax Saver**
>
> Where the gift is one of a business asset, you can elect jointly with the transferee for payment of the tax on the gift to be postponed until the asset is subsequently disposed of by the transferee.

Short life assets

Short life, or wasting, assets are those with an expected lifespan of less than 50 years. A gain on the disposal of a wasting asset is worked out in the same way as that on the disposal of any other asset, except that the purchase price wastes away during the expected lifespan of the asset.

Leases of land for less than 50 years are wasting assets. There is a specific formula for calculating the proportion of the purchase price of a lease that can be deducted from the sale proceeds.

The gain or loss on the sale of a wasting asset that is also 'tangible moveable property' is outside of tax.

Part disposals

There are several points to be aware of when you dispose of only part of an asset you own.

- You apportion the acquisition cost between the part sold and the fraction retained. This is worked out on a pro-rata basis by reference to the sale proceeds of the part sold and the open-market value of the proportion retained.

- The proportion of the cost price of the asset attributable to the part retained can be set against the proceeds on the sale of the remainder at a later date.

- If the part sold is small compared with the value of the whole asset, you can simply deduct the sale proceeds from the acquisition cost. Where the part disposal is one of land, this procedure can be followed so long as the sale proceeds are less than both £20,000 and one-fifth of the value of the remaining land.

Enterprise Investment Scheme

A profit on disposing of qualifying shares under the Enterprise Investment Scheme (EIS) is free of Capital Gains Tax, provided:

- the Income Tax relief originally allowed on the investment has not been withdrawn; and

- the disposal takes place at least three years after the issue of the shares.

If you incur a loss on disposing of qualifying shares you can offset the loss, after taking off any Income Tax relief allowed, against either:

- capital gains in the same year that the loss is realized; or
- your taxable income in the year of loss, or the previous year.

It is also possible to defer Capital Gains Tax payable on chargeable gains by reinvesting the gains in qualifying EIS shares. For deferral relief purposes the chargeable gains must be reinvested in the period beginning one year before, and ending three years after, the original disposal. Deferral relief can be claimed:

- along with both Income Tax relief (see Chapter 10) and exemption from Capital Gains Tax (as above) up to an annual investment limit of £1 million;
- on its own as the amount of gains that can be deferred is unlimited; or
- in any other combination you choose within the rules.

If deferral relief is claimed, the original liability to Capital Gains Tax will crystallize when the EIS shares are sold.

Seed Enterprise Investment Scheme

A gain on disposing of shares qualifying under the Seed Enterprise Investment Scheme (SEIS) is not chargeable to Capital Gains Tax provided:

- the Income Tax Relief granted on the investment has not been withdrawn; and
- the disposal does not occur within three years after the shares have been issued.

Tax Saver

You can claim exemption from Capital Gains Tax on half of your capital gains up to a maximum of £100,000 where the profit is re-invested in a SEIS. As a consequence, the maximum gains free of Capital Gains Tax are £50,000.

Venture Capital Trusts

A profit on disposal of shares in a Venture Capital Trust (VCT) is exempt from Capital Gains Tax provided:

- the original subscription for the shares disposed of did not exceed the maximum permitted investment limit in the year of purchase, £200,000 for 2021/22; and
- the company qualifies as a VCT both at the time the shares are acquired and at the date of disposal.

Inheritances

No Capital Gains Tax is payable on the unrealized profits on your assets as at the date of your death. When you inherit an asset you acquire it at the value on the date of death of the deceased. Generally, this rule is also applied whenever you become entitled to assets from a Trust.

14

How to complete your Tax Return and work out your tax

This tax guide is being published shortly after HMRC have sent out emails, letters or Tax Returns:

- requiring taxpayers, by law, to make a Return of their taxable income and capital gains for the year from 6 April 2021 to 5 April 2022; and
- to claim the allowances and tax reliefs to which they are entitled for the same year.

Do I need to complete a Tax Return?

You probably don't need to complete a Tax Return if:

- your tax affairs are not complicated; and
- you receive income taxed under PAYE.

But you may need to fill one in if:

- your tax affairs are not straightforward; and
- you receive income from several sources.

Who has to complete a Tax Return?

HMRC will want a Tax Return from you each year if you:

- earn more than £50,000 and either you, your wife or partner is receiving Child Benefit;
- are self-employed and earn more than £1,000;
- are a company director;

- own land or property in the United Kingdom from which you receive rental income;

- have other untaxed income and it is not possible to collect the tax due through your PAYE tax code;

- make capital gains in excess of the annual exemption limit; or

- are an employee or pensioner with more complex tax affairs.

Employees and pensioners with complex tax affairs

You must fill in a Tax Return if you:

- have an annual salary or pension of at least £100,000;

- receive income from savings or investments of at least £10,000 (before tax) in a year;

- hold shares on which the annual dividends are £10,000 or more (before tax) annually;

- have untaxed income in excess of £2,500; or

- owe tax at the end of the year that cannot be collected in the following year through your PAYE tax code.

How do I register for Self Assessment?

HMRC is strongly recommending and encouraging taxpayers to file online because:

- it is secure and convenient;

- tax calculations are done for you automatically;

- on-screen help is available if you need it;

- you get an immediate acknowledgement that your Return has been received; and

- if you are owed money, you will get a faster repayment.

You can also:

- see whether HMRC owe you money, or how much you owe HMRC;

- view your statement of account for the last three years;

- make changes to your personal contact details; and
- make a claim to reduce payments on account or request a refund (if your account is in credit).

You need to visit the GOV.UK website at www.gov.uk/register-for-self-assessment:

- if you are not already registered for Self Assessment; and
- to file your Tax Return online with HMRC's free online service.

You must register by 5 October 2022 if you have to file a Tax Return for 2021/22. Should you miss this deadline you may become liable to a penalty. You will need:

- your NINO; and
- information about your business (if applicable).

At the end of the registration process, HMRC will give you a Unique Taxpayer Reference (UTR).

To file a Tax Return online you need an HMRC online account. If you are not given an account when you register you can sign up for one through HMRC's online services.

Filing deadlines

The deadline for filing your 2021/22 Tax Return online is 31 January 2023. If you decide to complete a paper Tax Return for 2021/22 you must send it back by 31 October 2022 so HMRC has time:

- to work out the tax you owe or the refund due to you; and
- to let you know the result of their calculation before the 31 January 2022 payment deadline.

Tax Saver

Unless your preference is to make a direct payment by 31 January 2023, HMRC will, if possible, collect the tax you owe for the year through next year's tax code so long as they either:

- receive your paper 2021/22 Tax Return by 31 October 2022; or
- you file online by 31 December 2022

and you:

- owe tax of not more than £3,000; and
- have a PAYE tax code.

There is no interest or other charge for spreading out the tax under payment for 2021/22 over income received in 2023/24.

The Tax Return

The Tax Return runs to eight pages. Also available from HMRC are:

- a Tax Return guide;
- supplementary colour-coded pages based on your tax history; and
- a separate four-page section of Additional Information pages for dealing with the less common types of income and tax reliefs.

The list of the various supplementary pages is as follows:

Employment	Pink
Self-employment	Orange
Partnership	Turquoise
UK property	Red
Foreign	Mustard
Trusts etc	Brown
Capital gains summary	Blue
Residence, remittance basis, etc	Green

Getting started

Try to avoid the temptation of putting off the job of filling in your Return. It is better to get on with it as soon as you can because you will:

- have more time to get help from HMRC if you need it;
- have more time to save for any tax you owe; and
- get a big weight off your mind!

Tax Saver

Getting started as soon as possible is a must if you have paid too much tax. HMRC will refund any overpayment direct to your bank or building society. This is the safest and quickest method. Always fill in boxes 4–14 on page TR6 as appropriate.

Start by going to page TR2. This will help you decide which, if any, supplementary pages you need. These can be obtained by:

- telephoning the order line on 0300 200 3610 (open seven days a week from 8 am to 10 pm); or
- going to www.gov.uk/self-assessment-forms-and-helpsheets to download them.

The supplementary pages come with notes to help you fill in the pages you requested. Helpsheets, explanatory booklets and leaflets that may also further assist you in working out the income or capital gains to be declared are similarly available from HMRC, and listed in Appendix 6.

Keeping proper records

Tax Saver

First and foremost, keep proper and orderly records as:

- this will make it easier for you to complete your Tax Return fully and accurately; and
- if the tax office decides to enquire into your Tax Return you will be able to demonstrate that the Return is both accurate and complete from the records you have maintained.

Before you start filling in your Tax Return you need to gather together all the information on your income, capital gains, reliefs and allowances from the records you have been keeping for the year to 5 April 2022. For most types of income and capital gains you only need to retain the records given to you by whoever provided that income or realized the gains for you. This means for those of you:

- In employment:
  - your Form P60, a certificate your employer will give you after 5 April (the end of the tax year) detailing your pay and the tax deducted from it;
  - Form P11D or P9D or equivalent information from your employer showing any benefits-in-kind and expenses payments you received;
  - any Form P45 (part 1A) certificate from an employer showing pay and tax from a job you have left;
  - any Form P160 (part 1A) you may have been given when you retire and then go on to receive a pension from your former employer;
  - your payslips or pay statements;
  - a note of the amount of any tips or gratuities along with details of any other taxable receipts. You are well advised to note these as soon as possible after you receive them, and not simply estimate them at the end of the year.
- Receiving a UK pension or Social Security benefits:
  - your Form P60, a certificate given to you by the payer of your occupational pension, stating the amount of your pension and the tax deducted;
  - a certificate detailing any other pension you received and the tax deducted from it;
  - information given to you by the Department for Work and Pensions (DWP) relating to state pensions, taxable state benefits, Statutory Sick, Maternity or Paternity Pay and the Jobseeker's Allowance.
- In business:
  - this is dealt with in the section on records in Chapter 7.
- Letting out property:
  - the dates when your property is rented;
  - all the rents you receive;
  - bills and invoices for all the allowable expenses you incur to run and manage your property.
- Receiving investment income:
  - bank and building society statements, passbooks and tax deduction certificates;

- statements of interest and any other income received from your savings and investments; for example, an annuity;

- vouchers for dividends received from UK companies;

- unit trust tax vouchers;

- life insurance chargeable event certificates;

- details of any income you received from a trust or the estate of a deceased person;

- information about any exceptional amounts – such as an inheritance or other windfall – that you receive and subsequently invest.

- Making capital gains or losses:

  - contracts for the purchase or sale of shares, unit trusts, property or any other assets;

  - copies of any valuations you need to work out your capital gains or losses;

  - bills, invoices or other evidence of payment records such as bank statements and cheque stubs for costs you claim for the purchase, improvement or sale of assets;

  - details of any assets you have given away or put into a trust.

- Claiming personal allowances, other deductions or reliefs:

  - certificates of interest paid on any loans that qualify for tax relief;

  - declarations you have made to charities of gifts under Gift Aid;

  - receipts for the payment of pension premiums;

  - notification that you are registered as a blind person.

This list of the types of records you are advised to keep is not exhaustive and does not cover every situation. If you are in any doubt, ask your tax office for assistance.

Tax Saver

Always remember to keep your records for the right length of time. This is:

- the fifth anniversary of 31 January following the tax year if you are self-employed, in partnership or letting property; and

- in any other case the first 31 January anniversary after the tax year.

Filling in your Tax Return

The paper Tax Return is designed to be read by a machine. It is important to complete the form properly so that it is correctly read.

Tax Saver

Always:

- use black ink and capital letters;
- cross out any mistakes and write the correct information below;
- enter figures in whole pounds, ignoring pence;
- round down income;
- round up expenses and tax paid – this will benefit you;
- write in the spaces provided; and
- if a box does not apply simply leave it blank.

There is not enough space to reproduce the eight-page Tax Return, as well as the Additional Information and supplementary pages. In the following pages, you will find reproductions of the supplementary page on Employment, most of the sections for the Tax Return and some of those from the Additional Information pages. All of these have been sourced from HMRC.

If you have more than one job you will need to fill in a separate employment page for each job as follows.

- In Box 1 enter your before-tax salary or wage from your P60 or P45.
- Enter the tax taken off your pay in Box 2.
- Tips and other payments not on your P60 go in Box 3.
- The PAYE tax reference of your employer, which will be shown on your P60 or P45, needs to be entered in Box 4.
- Box 5 is for your employer's name.
- Use your Form P11D, or equivalent information, to enter the taxable amounts of any benefits from your employment in Boxes 9 to 16.

- Any business travel or subsistence expenses, professional fees and subscriptions and other expenses paid by you and on which you can claim tax relief go in Boxes 17 to 20.

Leaving aside the sections on the first two pages of the Tax Return asking for your personal details, the first part of page TR3 is for you to report your interest and dividend income as follows.

- You may have received interest where tax has been taken off at source. If so, enter the after-tax figure in Box 1.

- In Box 2 you should enter the total of the amounts of interest on all your UK bank, building society and other interest-bearing accounts where no tax has been deducted.

- If you have received any interest from overseas not exceeding £2,000, then this amount goes in Box 3.

- The total of all your dividends in the year should be entered in Box 4.

- You should do likewise in completing Box 5 in respect of any dividends received from authorized unit trusts and open-ended investment companies.

- Boxes 6 and 7 are for your foreign dividends, up to £300, and the tax taken off these foreign dividends.

The next section on page TR3 deals with UK pensions, annuities and other State benefits received as follows.

- The figure to put in Box 8 is the total of your weekly entitlements to the State Pension, even if you were paid monthly or quarterly. If you are unsure about the amount, telephone the Pension Direct Service on 0345 606 0265 and ask for this figure for the year from 6 April 2021 to 5 April 2022. Do not include either the Christmas bonus or your winter fuel payment as these are not taxable.

- You will only need to complete Boxes 9 and 10 if you received a State Pension lump sum in the year.

- All your other pension income, and the tax taken off, needs to be shown in Boxes 11 and 12. In Box 19 on page 7 you should separately list the names of the payers of your pensions, the amounts paid and the tax deducted.

- The remaining boxes are relevant if you are receiving Incapacity Benefit, contribution-based Employment and Support Allowance, Jobseeker's Allowance or other benefits that are taxable.

Figure 14.1

HM Revenue & Customs

Employment
Tax year 6 April 2021 to 5 April 2022 (2021 to 22)

Your name	Your Unique Taxpayer Reference (UTR)
TOM SMITH	4 3 2 9 6 5 5 4 3 4

For help filling in this form, go to www.gov.uk/taxreturnforms and read the notes and helpsheets.

Complete an 'Employment' page for each employment or directorship

1 Pay from this employment – the total from your P45 or P60 – before tax was taken off
£ 3 7 4 4 0 . 0 0

2 UK tax taken off pay in box 1
£ − 8 5 5 3 . 0 0

3 Tips and other payments not on your P60
£ . 0 0

4 PAYE tax reference of your employer (on your P45/P60)
2 8 / B 6 0 4

5 Your employer's name
BROADWOOD ENGINEERS LTD

6 If you were a company director, put 'X' in the box

6.1 If you ceased being a director before 6 April 2020, put the date the directorship ceased in the box DD MM YYYY

7 And, if the company was a close company, put 'X' in the box

8 If you're a part-time teacher in England or Wales and are on the Repayment of Teachers' Loans Scheme for this employment, put 'X' in the box

8.1 If box 1 includes any disguised remuneration income, put 'X' in the box - read the notes

Benefits from your employment – use your form P11D (or equivalent information)

9 Company cars and vans
£ 4 0 0 0 . 0 0

10 Fuel for company cars and vans
£ 4 5 2 0 . 0 0

11 Private medical and dental insurance
£ 9 0 0 . 0 0

12 Vouchers, credit cards and excess mileage allowance
£ . 0 0

13 Goods and other assets provided by your employer
£ . 0 0

14 Accommodation provided by your employer
£ . 0 0

15 Other benefits (including interest-free and low interest loans)
£ . 0 0

16 Expenses payments received and balancing charges
£ . 0 0

Employment expenses

17 Business travel and subsistence expenses
£ . 0 0

18 Fixed deductions for expenses
£ . 0 0

19 Professional fees and subscriptions
£ . 0 0

20 Other expenses and capital allowances
£ . 0 0

SOURCE HMRC

Figure 14.2

Interest and dividends from UK banks, building societies etc

1	Taxed UK interest etc - the net amount after tax has been taken off - read the notes
	£ 8 0 · 0 0
2	Untaxed UK interest etc - amounts which have not had tax taken off - read the notes
	£ 2 4 0 · 0 0
3	Untaxed foreign interest (up to £2,000) - amounts which have not had tax taken off - read the notes
	£ · 0 0
4	Dividends from UK companies - the amount received - read the notes
	£ 1 5 8 0 · 0 0
5	Other dividends - the amount received - read the notes
	£ 1 9 0 · 0 0
6	Foreign dividends (up to £300) - the amount in sterling after foreign tax was taken off. Do not include this amount in the 'Foreign' pages
	£ 1 6 0 · 0 0
7	Tax taken off foreign dividends - the sterling equivalent
	£ 2 4 · 0 0

SOURCE HMRC

Figure 14.3

UK pensions, annuities and other state benefits received

8	State Pension - amount you were entitled to receive in the year, **not the weekly or 4-weekly amount** - read the notes
	£ 6 5 5 0 · 0 0
9	State Pension lump sum - the gross amount of any lump sum - read the notes
	£ · 0 0
10	Tax taken off box 9
	£ · 0 0
11	Pensions (other than State Pension), retirement annuities and taxable triviality payments - the gross amount. Tax taken off goes in box 12
	£ 2 1 0 0 0 · 0 0
12	Tax taken off box 11
	£ — 3 1 4 0 · 0 0
13	Taxable Incapacity Benefit and contribution-based Employment and Support Allowance - read the notes
	£ · 0 0
14	Tax taken off Incapacity Benefit in box 13
	£ · 0 0
15	Jobseeker's Allowance
	£ · 0 0
16	Total of any other taxable State Pensions and benefits
	£ · 0 0

SOURCE HMRC

The final section on page TR3 is for reporting other UK income not included on the supplementary pages and, in most cases, is unlikely to be relevant to your circumstances.

Page TR4 is devoted to tax reliefs, the first part of which is relevant if you want to claim relief for pension contributions. It is likely that the only boxes you will need to complete are Boxes 1 and 2.

Figure 14.4

Paying into registered pension schemes and overseas pension schemes

Do not include payments you make to your employer's pension scheme which are deducted from your pay before tax or payments made by your employer. If your contributions and other pension inputs are more than the Annual Allowance, you should also fill in boxes 10, 11 and 12 on page Ai 4 of the 'Additional information' pages.

1 Payments to registered pension schemes where basic rate tax relief will be claimed by your pension provider (called 'relief at source'). Enter the payments and basic rate tax	3 Payments to your employer's scheme which were not deducted from your pay before tax - this will be unusual - read the notes
£ 4 4 0 0 · 0 0	£ · 0 0
2 Payments to a retirement annuity contract where basic rate tax relief will not be claimed by your provider	4 Payments to an overseas pension scheme, which is not UK-registered, which are eligible for tax relief and were not deducted from your pay before tax
£ 1 8 0 0 · 0 0	£ · 0 0

SOURCE HMRC

If you pay tax at the higher or additional rates you will be entitled to tax relief on the difference between either 40 per cent or 45 per cent and the basic rate of 20 per cent on your donations to charities under Gift Aid. However, even if you are not claiming this tax relief you should complete the part of the Return on charitable giving as follows.

- The total of all your Gift Aid payments goes in Box 5.

- In Box 6 you need to enter the total of any 'one-off' payments in the figure in Box 5.

- Any Gift Aid donations made in 2021/22 and related back to 2020/21 go in Box 7.

- Perhaps by the time you fill in your Tax Return and send it back to your tax office you have made donations under Gift Aid in the 2022/23 tax year. You can elect to have those payments treated as though they were made in the year to 5 April 2022. Enter the figure in Box 8.

- The value of any shares or securities, land and buildings that you have gifted to charity in the year should be entered in Boxes 9 and 10 respectively.

In Boxes 11 and 12 you should respectively state:

- the value of any investments gifted to non-UK charities in Boxes 9 and 10; and

- Gift Aid payments to non-UK charities in Box 5.

Figure 14.5

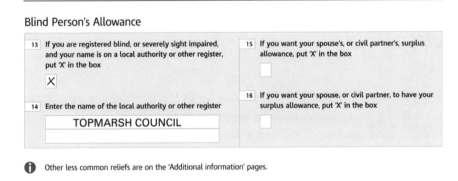

Charitable giving

5	Gift Aid payments made in the year to 5 April 2022 £ 1 7 9 0 · 0 0	**9**	Value of qualifying shares or securities gifted to charity £ 3 7 8 0 · 0 0
6	Total of any 'one-off' payments in box 5 £ 1 3 5 0 · 0 0	**10**	Value of qualifying land and buildings gifted to charity £ · 0 0
7	Gift Aid payments made in the year to 5 April 2022 but treated as if made in the year to 5 April 2021 £ 6 2 0 · 0 0	**11**	Value of qualifying investments gifted to non-UK charities in boxes 9 and 10 £ · 0 0
8	Gift Aid payments made after 5 April 2022 but to be treated as if made in the year to 5 April 2022 £ 7 8 0 · 0 0	**12**	Gift Aid payments to non-UK charities in box 5 £ · 0 0

SOURCE HMRC

The next tax relief section on page TR4 is only of relevance to you if you can make a claim for the special blind person's allowance. You need to give the name of the local authority, or equivalent body, with whom you have registered your blindness.

Figure 14.6

Blind Person's Allowance

13	If you are registered blind, or severely sight impaired, and your name is on a local authority or other register, put 'X' in the box X	**15**	If you want your spouse's, or civil partner's, surplus allowance, put 'X' in the box
14	Enter the name of the local authority or other register TOPMARSH COUNCIL	**16**	If you want your spouse, or civil partner, to have your surplus allowance, put 'X' in the box

ⓘ   Other less common reliefs are on the 'Additional information' pages.

SOURCE HMRC

Page TR5 is concerned with:

- Student Loan repayments;
- High Income Child Benefit Charge; and
- the Marriage Allowance.

You will only need to complete the High Income Child Benefit Charge section if:

- your income was over £50,000 in 2021/22;

- you or your spouse/partner received Child Benefit in the year to 5 April 2021; and

- for couples only – your income was more than that of your spouse/partner.

Figure 14.7

Marriage Allowance

Please read the notes. If your income for the year ended 5 April 2021 was less than £12,570 you can transfer £1,260 of your Personal Allowance to your spouse or civil partner to reduce the amount of tax they pay if all of the following apply:
- you were married to, or in a civil partnership with, the same person for all or part of the tax year
- you were both born on or after 6 April 1935
- your spouse or civil partner's income was not taxed at the higher rate

Fill in this section if you want to make the transfer:

1 Your spouse or civil partner's first name	4 Your spouse or civil partner's date of birth DD MM YYYY
TOM	06 08 1952

2 Your spouse or civil partner's last name	5 Date of marriage or civil partnership DD MM YYYY
SMITH	19 05 1978

3 Your spouse or civil partner's National Insurance number	
BZ 62 24 17 A	

SOURCE HMRC

Perhaps your income in 2021/22 was under £12,570? If so, you can cut the tax bill of your spouse/partner by transferring £1,260 of your personal allowance to them. But to do so all of the following must apply.

- You were both born after 5 April 1935.

- You were married to, or in a civil partnership with, the same person for all or part of 2021/22.

- The income of your spouse or civil partner in 2019/20 was no more than £50,270.

Figure 14.8

High Income Child Benefit Charge

Fill in this section if all of the following apply:

• your income was over £50,000
• you or your partner (if you have one) got Child Benefit (this also applies if someone else claims Child Benefit for a child who lives with you and pays you or your partner for the child's upkeep)
• couples only - your income was higher than your partner's

Please read the notes. Use the calculator at www.gov.uk/child-benefit-tax-calculator to help you work out the Child Benefit payments you received.

If you have to pay this charge for the 2021-22 tax year and you do not want us to use your 2021-22 PAYE tax code to collect that tax during the year, put 'X' in box 3 on page TR 6.

1 Enter the total amount of Child Benefit you and your partner got for the year to 5 April 2021	3 Enter the date that you and your partner stopped getting all Child Benefit payments if this was before 6 April 2021
£ 1 7 8 8 · 0 0	DD MM YYYY
2 Enter the number of children you and your partner got Child Benefit for on 5 April 2021	
2	

SOURCE HMRC

Before you finish off your Tax Return, you should look at the Additional Information pages, which are for:

• less common types of income; and

• other tax reliefs and information.

In particular, the second section on page Ai2 is for you to claim other tax reliefs, such as the following.

• Your subscriptions for new ordinary shares in a Venture Capital Trust go in Box 1.

• Box 2 is for your subscriptions for shares issued under the Enterprise Investment Scheme.

• The total of your qualifying loan interest payable in the year should be entered in Box 5.

• Maintenance or alimony payments you are making, subject to a maximum of £3,260, should be entered in Box 7, but only if you or your former spouse or civil partner was born before 6 April 1935.

• In Box 10 you should put the amount of your subscriptions for shares under the Seed Enterprise Investment Scheme.

Figure 14.9

Other tax reliefs – read the notes

1	Subscriptions for Venture Capital Trust shares – the amount on which relief is claimed
	£ [ ] [ ] [ ] [ ] 4 0 0 0 · 0 0

2	Subscriptions for shares under the Enterprise Investment Scheme – the amount on which relief is claimed
	£ [ ] [ ] [ ] 2 9 2 0 · 0 0

3	Community Investment Tax Relief – the amount on which relief is claimed
	£ [ ] [ ] [ ] [ ] [ ] [ ] [ ] · 0 0

4	Annual payments made
	£ [ ] [ ] [ ] [ ] [ ] [ ] [ ] · 0 0

5	Qualifying loan interest payable in the year
	£ [ ] [ ] [ ] [ ] 8 3 0 · 0 0

6	Post-cessation trade relief and certain other losses
	£ [ ] [ ] [ ] [ ] [ ] [ ] [ ] · 0 0

7	Maintenance payments (up to £3,530) – if you or your former spouse or civil partner were born before 6 April 1935
	£ [ ] 2 8 1 0 · 0 0

8	Payments to a trade union for death benefits – half the amount paid (maximum £100)
	£ [ ] [ ] [ ] [ ] · 0 0

9	Relief claimed on a qualifying distribution on the redemption of bonus shares or securities
	£ [ ] [ ] [ ] [ ] [ ] [ ] [ ] · 0 0

10	Subscriptions for shares under the Seed Enterprise Investment Scheme
	£ [ ] [ ] [ ] 1 3 4 0 · 0 0

11	Social Investment Tax Relief – the amount on which relief is claimed
	£ [ ] [ ] [ ] [ ] [ ] [ ] [ ] · 0 0

12	Non-deductible loan interest from investments into property partnerships not included in box 5
	£ [ ] [ ] [ ] [ ] [ ] [ ] [ ] · 0 0

SOURCE HMRC

Then follows a section on the married couple's allowance. You should carefully read the notes at the top of page Ai3 before completing Boxes 1 to 11 as appropriate.

The second part of this page is devoted to Income Tax losses and the limit of Income Tax relief on these losses (see Chapter 7).

You are probably now in a position to put the finishing touches to your Tax Return. If you want to calculate your tax you will have to ask HMRC for the Tax Calculation Summary, notes and helpsheets that will assist you in working out:

- any tax due or repayable; and

- if payments on account are necessary.

There is a choice of boxes to complete on page TR6 if you have not paid enough tax.

- Box 2 covers tax due for 2021/22 and the alternative methods of payment if you owe less than £3,000.

- Box 3 deals with the collection of tax for 2022/23 on your savings income and/or the High Income Child Benefit Charge.

But if you have overpaid you need to give the information requested in Boxes 4 to 14 on page TR6 of the bank or building society account into which you would like the tax refund paid.

Do not miss the deadline for filing your Tax Return because, perhaps, you are waiting for some final figures. Use estimates and make sure you send the correct figures as soon as you can. You should tick Box 20 on page TR8 of your Return and describe in the space provided at Box 19:

- which figures are provisional (you should refer to the appropriate box numbers on your Tax Return or any other supplementary pages you have completed);
- why you could not give final figures; and
- when you expect to be able to provide your tax office with the correct information.

Put 'X' in Box 21 if you are enclosing separate supplementary pages. You must then sign and date the Return in Box 22. Have regard to the wording of the declaration:

> I declare the information I've given on this tax return and any supplementary pages is correct and complete to the best of my knowledge and belief. I understand that I may have to pay financial penalties and face prosecution if I give false information.

The form and any supplementary pages are now ready to send back to your tax office.

Working out your tax

The key steps in calculating your tax bill are as follows.

1 Add up all the non-savings income you have entered on your Return.

2 Total the allowances and other deductions you have claimed for the year but excluding those such as personal pension premiums and donations under Gift Aid paid net of tax at the basic rate.

3 Take (2) away from (1).

4 Work out the tax due on (3) but increasing the basic rate band of £37,699 by the grossed up equivalent of personal pension and Gift Aid payments.

5 Add up your savings income for the year. Take into account the Personal Savings Allowance and calculate the tax on the balance.

6 Do the same for your dividend income, not forgetting the dividend allowance.

7 Add (4), (5) and (6) together.

8 If you are self-employed or in partnership, work out how much you owe for Classes 2 and 4 National Insurance Contributions.

9 Add (7) and (8) together and take away all tax deducted at source.

This is your tax bill unless you also owe tax on capital gains realized in excess of your annual exemption limit. You will then be able to:

- work out what tax you have to pay for 2021/22 due on 31 January 2023; and

- calculate any payments on account for 2022/23 payable on 31 January and 31 July 2023.

Illustration

Celia Mercer, who is single, is employed as a fashion designer. She frequently has to travel so her employer provides her with a company car, fuel for private mileage as well as private medical insurance cover.

In her spare time Celia speaks at trade shows. She also writes articles for fashion magazines.

A few years ago Celia's mother died. The inheritance she received is invested in a portfolio of shares. She also owns a buy-to-let flat and has spare cash deposited in building society accounts.

Celia filed her Tax Return for the year to 5 April 2022 online on 24 November 2022. It shows the following entries:

	£	Page no	Box no
(1) Employment			
Salary	64,000	E1	1
Tax deducted by employer	18,240	E1	2
Company car benefit	4,200	E1	9
Car fuel benefit	4,914	E1	10
Medical insurance	800	E1	11

(continued)

(Continued)

(2) Self-employment			
Adjusted profit shown by the accounts for the year to 30 September 2021	9,940	SEF4	76
(3) UK property			
Net rental income from buy-to-let flat	4,500	UKP2	38
(4) UK interest and dividends			
Building society interest	1,200	TR3	2
Dividends from UK companies	1,620	TR3	4
(5) Reliefs			
Personal pension premiums	2,200	TR4	1
Interest on loan to buy investment flat	3,100	Ai2	5
(6) Capital gains on share sales			
In excess of annual exemption limit	2,600	CG1	8

The calculation of Celia's tax liability for 2021/22 is as follows:

	£	£	£
Income received (before tax taken off)			
Pay, business profits and letting income	88,354		
Interest received from UK banks and building societies	700		
Dividends from UK companies	–		
Total income received		89,054	
Less:			
Personal allowance	12,570		
Total		12,570	
Total income on which tax is due		76,484	
Tax thereon:			
Pay, business profit and letting income		40,450 @ 20 per cent	8,090.00
		38,784 @ 40 per cent	15,513.60
Bank and building society interest		700 @ 40 per cent	280.00
Income Tax charged			23,883.60

(continued)

(Continued)

	£	£	£
Less:			
Tax deducted from salary		18,240.00	
Interest paid allowed at the basic rate £3,100 @ 20 per cent		620.00	18,860
			3,302.60
Add:			
Class 4 National Insurance Contributions		33.48	
capital Gains Tax: £2,600 @ 20 per cent		520.00	
			553.48
Tax due for 2021/22			5,577.08
Tax payments			
Tax due for 2021/22 (as above)			5,577.08
Payment on account made 31 January 2022			(1,200.00)
Payment on account made 31 July 2022			(1,200.00)
Balance due for 2021/22			3,177.08
Add:			
First payment on account for 2021/22			2,124.22
Amount due on 31 January 2022			5,301.30
Second payment on account for 2021/22			1,804.98
Amount due on 31 July 2022			3,496.32

Notes

(1) Celia's employment income comprises her salary of £64,000 and taxable benefits of £9,914.

(2) As a higher rate taxpayer Celia has a Personal Savings Allowance of £500. As a result she only has to pay tax on £700 of her building society interest of £1,200.

(3) Celia's dividends of £1,620 are all within the £2,000 dividend allowance.

(4) The band of income taxable at the basic rate is extended by the grossed up equivalent of the personal pension premiums of £2,200 from £37,500 by £2,750 to £40,250.

(5) Celia applied for, and was granted, permission to defer payment of her Class 2 National Insurance Contributions.

(6) The amount due for Class 4 Contributions is £33.48, being 9 per cent of £372 (£9,940 – threshold of £9,568).

(7) Tax payments of £1,200 were made by Celia on both 31 January and 31 July 2022 based on her tax liability for 2020/21.

(8) In working out her payments on account for 2022/23 Celia does not need to include her Capital Gains Tax liability for 2021/22 of £520.

What HMRC do

When your completed Tax Return is received by your tax office it will be processed as quickly as possible based on your entries on the Return. Any simple straightforward mistakes will be corrected by HMRC and you will be told about them.

You will then be sent a calculation of your tax position if you have asked HMRC to work this out for you. Alternatively, if you have calculated your own tax bill and it is incorrect, HMRC will send you their tax calculation.

Some other hints on efficient tax compliance

Tax Saver

Always remember that both send-back dates of 31 October (for paper) and 31 January (online) are critical. You must stick to them otherwise you will come within the penalty regime for the late filing of the Return.

Tax Saver

If the amount of any of your sources of income is substantially different compared to the previous year, use the Additional Information box on page TR7 to explain the reason for the change.

Tax Saver

Do not forget to sign the Return. This is one of the most common mistakes that HMRC have found when processing Tax Returns.

Tax Saver

Remember that you can amend your Self Assessment at any time in the 12-month period after the latest 31 January deadline.

Tax Saver

Remember the key dates in the Self Assessment calendar, which are summarized in Appendix 7.

15
Paying your tax, interest and penalties

Under the Self Assessment tax system:

- there are specified dates each year when you must pay your tax; and
- you regularly receive a Statement of Account from HMRC detailing both tax recently paid and the next amount due.

Tax payment dates

The tax payment dates for 2021/22 are:

		Due date for tax payments on account	Due date for final balance
Rental income and untaxed investment income			
Business profits	50%	31/1/2022	31/1/2023
Unpaid PAYE (where not coded)	50%	31/1/2022	
Higher and additional rate tax on investment income (taxed at source)			
Capital Gains Tax		N/A	31/1/2023

The one exception to the rule requiring direct payment of tax to HMRC relates to employees or pensioners who owe less than £3,000 in tax. They can choose to have the amount collected monthly in the following year through the PAYE system:

- by filing a paper Return at their tax office no later than 31 October following the end of the tax year; or

- by filing online by 30 December after the end of the tax year.

Payments on account

Some taxpayers, mainly those who are self-employed, will make two payments on account of the tax due for a year on:

- 31 January in the tax year; and

- 31 July following the end of the tax year.

Payments on account are worked out by splitting into two equal amounts the tax paid for the previous tax year (after taking off tax incurred at source and any Capital Gains Tax).

You do not need to make payments on account of Income Tax if:

- the amount you owe for Income Tax and Class 4 National Insurance Contributions for the previous tax year, after taking off tax paid at source, is less than £1,000; or

- at least 80 per cent of your Income Tax and Class 4 National Insurance Contributions bill for the preceding tax year was represented by tax deducted from the income before you received it.

It follows that most employees and pensioners will not have to make the half-yearly payments on account.

Reduced payments on account

Maybe, because of a change in your financial circumstances, your payments on account for the tax year (based on what you paid in the previous year) point towards an overstatement of your likely liability for the year.

This might happen where you expect:

- your income in 2022/23 to be lower than that in 2021/22; or

- your allowances or reliefs to be higher; or

- that more of your income will incur tax at source, for example under PAYE, in 2021/22.

> **Tax Saver**
>
> In such circumstances you can claim to reduce your payments on account. You do this by using Form SA303, which is available online or from your tax office. The form gives guidance on how to complete it.

If the claim to reduce your payments on account subsequently turns out to be excessive then you will be asked to pay interest on the difference between the reduced tax you actually paid and the payments on account that should have been made.

Statements of Account

At the top of your Self Assessment Statement you will see:

- the Statement number and date of issue;
- your 10-digit Unique Taxpayer Reference number (UTR);
- your National Insurance Number (NINO); and
- your employer's tax reference, if you are employed.

The Statement then goes on to document:

- the opening balance, if any, brought forward from the previous Statement;
- what has happened since the last Statement; and
- whether there is an over-payment or, most probably, an amount to pay, and when to pay it. This is shown in a summary box at the end of the Statement.

If you are making payments on account you should expect to receive the following Statements up to February 2023:

July 2022	To tell you of the second payment on account for 2021/22 due on 31 July 2022.
August 2022	To let you know of any outstanding balance of the second payment on account. The statement will also include a figure for interest due to date.

(continued)

(Continued)

January 2023	To advise you of your balancing payment for 2021/22 and your first payment on account for 2022/23, both due on 31 January 2023.
February 2023	To show any outstanding amounts that should have been paid on 31 January 2023. The statement will also include a charge for interest due to date.

You should also receive a Statement of Account:

- whenever there is a change to the amount of tax you owe; and
- where you are due a refund from HMRC.

Other points of interest are:

- As HMRC carry out security checks, any tax refund due to you may not actually be issued until some time after the date shown on your Statement of Account.
- Where a tax liability will shortly be due for payment, HMRC will usually set any tax refund against this amount and then just repay the balance.
- If you have made a payment in the short period before you receive a Statement, it will appear on the next one.

If you have a Personal Tax Account or have registered for Self Assessment online you can access a wide range of services, including:

- viewing the latest issued copy of your Statement, as well as any Statements issued to you in the last three years;
- viewing payments/credits and how these have been allocated;
- viewing liabilities by tax year, including interest, penalties and surcharges;
- requesting repayments where an account is in credit;
- claiming to reduce payments on account;
- viewing and changing your address; and
- paying by direct debit online.

Paying your tax

There are a number of secure and efficient methods for paying your tax recommended by HMRC.

You can pay:

- using the internet or telephone;
- at your bank;
- by debit card online; or
- by direct debit. This service is available online. You have a choice of setting up either a Single Payment or a Budget Payment Plan.

Many of us:

- already use direct debit to make regular payments for household and other costs; and
- are familiar with the advantages of paying by direct debit.

Under the Budget Payment Plan, which is voluntary, you can make regular payments towards a future tax liability. The plan is flexible and you:

- decide the regular weekly or monthly amount you want to pay to HMRC;
- can choose to amend your regular payment amount;
- are free to take a break or suspend payment for a period of up to six months; and
- can cancel the Budget Payment Plan at any time.

The payments you make:

- are in advance; and
- reduce what you have to pay on either the following 31 January or 31 July.

You must still pay the full amount of tax by the due date.

If you use payment by post you should:

- make your cheque out to 'HM Revenue & Customs Only' followed by your Unique Taxpayer Reference; and
- send it to HMRC in the return envelope accompanied by the tear-off payment slip from your Statement of Account.

A stamp for the correct postage is needed. If you do not have a return envelope, your cheque should be sent to HMRC, Direct BX5 5BD.

HMRC politely request that:

- your cheque and the tear-off payment slip be unfolded;
- you do not staple or attach paperclips to cheques; and
- you do not pay your tax by sending cash through the post.

You can assist your accounts office in dealing promptly with your tax payment by:

- including a separate letter if you are sending a post-dated cheque, or want to give further information about your payment; and

- paying on time – you will not then incur interest charges.

Certificates of tax deposit

You can use a Certificate of Tax Deposit to settle a tax liability. The main features of such certificates are:

- tax deposits over £100,000 earn interest from the date of purchase to the normal due date for payment of the tax; and

- the interest is taxable.

However, they are no longer available to purchase.

Business Payment Support Service

Tax Saver

The Payment Support Service is dedicated to assisting businesses with temporary cash flow problems.

If you are concerned:

- about being able to meet tax, National Insurance or other payments due to HMRC; or

- that future payments could cause you difficulties,

you can get in touch with HMRC to discuss payment options.

You will be asked for the following information:

- your tax reference number;

- details of the tax that you are having or will have trouble paying; and

- an outline summary of the income and expenses of your business.

This will enable HMRC staff to review your particular circumstances and discuss temporary options relevant to the needs of your business, which could, for example, include allowing you to make tax payments over a longer period. You will not be charged late payment surcharges in such an arrangement although interest will continue to accrue on payments made beyond their due and payable date.

The number to telephone if you need assistance is 0300 200 3835.

What if I can't pay my tax?

If you are unable to settle your tax bill you should speak to the office which sent you the most recent communication. They should be able to help you by:

- giving you extra time to pay; or
- allowing you to settle it in instalments.

HMRC has several options when you fail to:

- reach an agreement; or
- maintain the payments you said you would make.

These are:

- collecting what you owe through your earnings or pension;
- taking money from either your bank or building society account;
- seizing most of your possessions for sale at auction;
- magistrates or County Court proceedings; or
- making you bankrupt.

Date of receipt

Tax payments are considered to be received by the accounts office as follows:

Payment method	Effective date of payment
Received by post (except below)	Day of receipt by HMRC
Received by post following a day when the office has been closed for whatever reason (including a weekend)	The day the office was first closed (for payments received on Monday, the effective date will be the previous Saturday)

(continued)

(Continued)

Payment method	Effective date of payment
Electronic Funds Transfer (EFT) – payment by BACS or CHAPS (Clearing House Automated Payment System)	One working day immediately before the date that the value is received (a working day is defined as a Bank of England working day)
Bank Giro	The date on which payment was made at the bank

Interest

You will be charged late payment interest:

- if you do not pay your tax when it is due; and
- on any penalties based on the overdue tax.

The interest is calculated from the date on which the tax becomes due and payable until payment is made.

The interest rate is Bank Base Rate plus 2.5 per cent. At the time of going to print this works out at 2.75 per cent. Tax relief on the interest is not allowed.

There may be circumstances when the imposition of interest would not be fair to you and can be justifiably contested. HMRC's Code of Practice (No 1) sets out the circumstances in which HMRC will consider setting aside a change to interest in overdue tax where there has been an undue delay on their part.

You will be paid interest, which is called repayment interest and is not taxable, by HMRC on overpayment of any of the following:

- payments on account of Income Tax;
- Income Tax and Capital Gains Tax; and
- any penalties imposed.

The formula for working out the interest rate on repayments is Bank Base Rate minus 1 per cent but with a minimum rate of 0.5 per cent.

Remission of tax

Arrears of Income Tax or Capital Gains Tax may be waived if they result from HMRC's failure to make proper and timely use of information supplied by:

- the taxpayer about his or her own income, capital gains or personal circumstances;
- an employer, where the information affects an employee's notice of coding; or
- the DWP about a taxpayer's retirement, disability or widow's State Pension.

The concession is normally only given where the taxpayer:

- could reasonably have believed that his or her tax affairs were in order; and
- is notified of the arrears by the end of the tax year following that in which it arose.

Late payment penalty

A late payment penalty is levied on the late payment of Income Tax, but not payments on account, or Capital Gains Tax as follows:

Tax unpaid by 3 March* (30 days after the tax was due)	5% of unpaid tax
Tax unpaid by 3 August* (5 months after the initial penalty was imposed)	Further 5% of tax unpaid
Tax unpaid by 3 February* (11 months after the initial penalty was imposed)	Further 5% of tax unpaid

*These dates will be one day earlier when 31 January falls in a leap year.

A penalty notice must be formally served on you by HMRC. You have 30 days in which to appeal against the notice if you think you have a reasonable excuse for the late payment of the tax. Your appeal might be successful:

- if there is clear evidence that your cheque was lost in the post; or
- in the event of serious illness.

Examples of circumstances where your appeal will be rejected are:

- cheques wrongly made out; and
- lack of funds other than for exceptional reasons.

Penalties

The main penalties under Self Assessment are:

Offence	Penalty
You do not submit a paper Tax Return to your tax office by 31 October after the end of the tax year	£100
You do not file online by 31 January after the end of the tax year	£100
Your Return is more than three months late	An automatic penalty of £10 a day up to a maximum of £900
Your Return is more than six months late	A tax geared penalty that is the greater of 5% of the tax due and £300
Your Return is still outstanding after a year	Another tax geared penalty that again is the greater of 5% of the tax due and £300
	In particularly serious cases a higher penalty of up to 100% of the tax due can be imposed.

It is important to note that the time limits for the imposition of these late filing penalties run from:

- 31 October for paper Returns; and
- 31 January for online filers.

Where taxpayers have a genuinely good excuse for missing the annual filing deadline for submitting Tax Returns, they can appeal against the automatic late filing penalty.

What may be accepted by HMRC as a reasonable excuse for late filing include:

- where the Tax Return was not received by the taxpayer;
- where the Tax Return was lost in the post or delayed because of:
  - a fire or flood at the post office where the Tax Return was handled;
  - prolonged industrial action within the post office; or
  - an unforeseen event that disrupted the postal services.
- where a taxpayer lost his or her tax records as a result of fire, flood or theft;

- serious illness; and

- death of a spouse, domestic partner or close relative.

HMRC will not agree the following as a reasonable excuse for being late:

- Tax Return too difficult;

- pressure of work;

- lack of information; or

- absence of reminders from HMRC.

The other penalties are:

Offence	Penalty
You do not receive a Tax Return and fail to notify HMRC of chargeability to tax within six months of the end of the tax year	Percentage of the tax payable: a) None if the failure is not deliberate b) 30% for a careless oversight c) 70% for a deliberate but not concealed failure d) 100% if the failure was both deliberate and concealed
Failure to maintain and keep records	Up to £3,000
Fraudulently or negligently claiming to reduce interim tax payments	Up to an amount equivalent to the difference between the tax paid and the tax that should have been paid

Generally, a penalty determination must be made, or proceedings commenced, within six years of the date on which the penalty was incurred. The rules allow for this period of time to be extended to any later date within three years of the final determination of the tax liability.

The penalty regime for errors on documents and Returns depends on:

- why you made the error; and

- how serious the reason was.

HMRC use penalties to stop individuals who do not take care with their tax affairs from gaining an unfair advantage. If you take reasonable care to get it right, HMRC will not charge a penalty where an error occurs. Some of the ways you can demonstrate you took reasonable care are:

- keeping accurate records and updating them regularly so you can make sure your Tax Returns are correct;

- saving your records should you need them at a later date;
- checking what the correct position is when you do not understand something or, alternatively, seeking advice from HMRC or a competent tax adviser; and
- telling HMRC as soon as possible about any error you discover after sending in a Tax Return or other document.

If you do not take reasonable care HMRC can penalize any errors, and penalties will be higher if the errors are deliberate.

What if you have to pay a penalty? HMRC will:

- Contact you to discuss your tax.
- Discuss the reason for the error – the more serious the reason, the higher the tax penalty can be.
- Reduce the penalty if you help them work out the correct tax due.
- Explain why they are issuing a penalty and send you a penalty notice. HMRC can substantially reduce any penalty due if you:
  - tell them about any errors without being prompted;
  - help them work out if any extra tax is due; and
  - allow them to check your figures.

The penalty is a percentage of the extra tax due and depends on why you made the error, as follows:

	Rate of penalty	
Reason	**Maximum**	**Minimum**
Reasonable care	No penalty	
Carelessness	30%	0%
Deliberate	70%	20%
Deliberate and concealed	100%	30%

You will have to pay the tax and any interest due, as well as the penalty.

If you incur a penalty because you failed to take reasonable care with your tax affairs, HMRC can suspend it for up to two years. In that time you need to get your systems right. If you then meet all the conditions laid down by HMRC the penalty will be cancelled.

You always have the right of appeal where you think that a penalty is unfair.

16
Elections and claims: time limits

You will already have gathered that certain options available to you as a taxpayer are dependent on you submitting an election or making a claim to HMRC. As these will usually involve a saving in tax it is important to appreciate that you often need to act within prescribed time limits. This chapter brings together those elections and claims that are most likely to be of relevance to you. It also sets out the time limit for submission to HMRC. It is by no means exhaustive.

Chapter 2 – Tax rates and allowances

Election/claim	Time limit
The various elections for the transfer of the married couple's and blind person's allowances	Generally, before the start of the tax year for which it is to have effect
Claim to the personal allowances detailed in the chapter	No later than four years after 31 January next following the end of the tax year
Transfer of excess allowances between spouses/civil partners	No later than four years after 31 January next following the end of the tax year

Chapter 3 – Tax credits

Election/claim	Time limit
Claims for tax credits	Claims will only be backdated by a maximum of one month
Annual renewal	By 31 July following the end of a tax year

Chapter 4 – Interest payments and other outgoings

Election/claim	Time limit
Election to treat charity donations under Gift Aid as made in the previous tax year	On or before when you deliver your Tax Return for the previous year after the tax year

Chapter 6 – Value Added Tax

Election/claim	Time limit
Application for registration	No later than 30 days from the end of the month after the one when turnover exceeds the registration limit
Claim for bad debt relief	When a debt remains unpaid for more than six months

Chapter 7 – Working for yourself

Election/claim	Time limit
Cash accounting for a small business	Tick box on page SEF1 of the Tax Return
£1,000 small business income allowance	No later than one year after 31 January next following the tax year for the claim
Relief for post-cessation expenses	No later than one year after 31 January next following the tax year in which the payments are made
Creating a separate pool to work out the capital allowances on an asset with a short life expectancy	No later than one year after 31 January next following the tax year in which the period of account ended in which the expenditure is incurred
Relief for the loss sustained in the tax year against other income of the same year or the preceding year	Within one year after 31 January next following the tax year in which the loss arose
Relief for a trading loss against the profits arising from the same trade in subsequent periods	Within four years after 31 January next following the tax year in which the loss was sustained

(continued)

(Continued)

Election/claim	Time limit
Relief for the loss in the first four years of assessment of a new business to be given against the income of the three preceding years of assessment	No later than one year after 31 January next following the tax year in which the loss occurred
Relief for trading losses to be offset against capital gains	No later than one year after 31 January next following the tax year
Relief for the loss in the last 12 months of trading to be given against the profits of the same trade that were assessed in the three tax years prior to the year in which the trade was discontinued	Within four years after 31 January next following the tax year in which the trade ceased

Chapter 10 – Savings and investment income

Election/claim	Time limit
To claim a repayment of tax on your savings income	Within four years after the end of the tax year for which you are claiming
£1,000 small property income allowance	No later than one year after 31 January next following the tax year for the claim
An election to opt out of rent-a-room relief for a particular tax year, or withdrawal of an election	Within one year after 31 January next following the tax year
An election for the alternative basis of rent-a-room relief, or revocation of an election	Within one year after 31 January next following the tax year
Claim for Income Tax relief under the Enterprise Investment Scheme	Within four years after 31 January next following that in which the shares were issued
Claim for Income Tax relief under the Seed Enterprise Investment Scheme	Within four years after 31 January next following that in which the shares were issued
Declaration by a married couple or civil partners that their beneficial interest in joint property and the income arising from it are unequal	The date of the declaration, which must be sent to HMRC within 60 days

Chapter 13 – Capital gains

Election/claim	Time limit
Claim to the capital loss where the value of an asset becomes negligible	The loss arises on the date of claim although, in practice, a two-year period is allowed from the end of the tax year in which the asset became of negligible value
Claim for the loss on shares that were originally subscribed for in an unquoted trading company to be set against income in the year of loss, or the preceding year	No later than one year after 31 January next following the tax year in which the loss was made
Claim to Business Asset Disposal Relief	No later than one year after 31 January next following the tax year in which the disposal took place
An election to determine which of your homes is to be regarded as your principal residence for Capital Gains Tax purposes	Two years from the date when two or more properties are eligible

17
Inheritance Tax

Inheritance Tax is payable on:

- any chargeable transfers you make during your lifetime; and
- the value of your estate on death.

There are a number of exemptions and reliefs that, if optimized, can reduce the amount of tax payable, perhaps significantly.

As with all types of direct taxation, husband, wife and civil partners are all treated as separate individuals.

Inheritance Tax is administered by the Inheritance Tax Office of HMRC on 0300 123 1072, to whom all Returns and Accounts should be submitted.

Some of the aspects of the tax are complex, particularly those relating to:

- agricultural and business property; and
- transfers into Trusts.

What follows is a summary of the main areas of the tax that are likely to be of most relevance and interest to you.

Potentially exempt transfers

Perhaps the most significant feature of Inheritance Tax is that of a potentially exempt transfer (PET). This is:

- an outright gift to an individual;
- a gift into settlement for the benefit of a disabled person; or
- certain other transfers into Trust.

No tax is payable providing the donor survives for at least seven years from the date of making the gift.

Chargeable lifetime gifts

Any gift or transfer that is not potentially exempt is liable to Inheritance Tax when it is made. Typically, a gift into settlement is a chargeable lifetime transfer (CLT). In working out any Inheritance Tax due at the date of gift:

- it is only the excess, if any, over the nil rate band on which tax is payable; and
- the rate of tax is one-half of the rate applicable on death at the time.

Gifts with reservation and pre-owned assets

If you make a gift but carry on enjoying some benefit from the property or asset, it is still likely to be regarded as yours until either:

- the date when you stop enjoying any benefit from the gift; or
- your death.

This is what is known as a 'gift with reservation'.

You also have to pay Income Tax each year on the value of any assets that you continue to use or enjoy after you have given them away.

Exemptions

The main exemptions for individuals are:

- Transfers, without limit, between spouses/civil partners – both during lifetime and on death.
- Gifts up to £3,000 in any one tax year. Any part of the exemption that is unused can be carried forward, but to the following year only.

Nancy Young gave her brother £1,800 in August 2020. A year later, she wanted to make a more substantial gift, but this time to her sister. She was able to give away £4,200 in September 2021, within her annual exemption limits for 2020/21 and 2021/22 as follows:

	£
2020/21	
Annual exemption limit	3,000
Less: Gift to brother	1,800
Carried forward to next year	1,200
2021/22	
Annual exemption limit	3,000
Add: Exemption unused in 2020/21	1,200
Available exemption for the year	4,200
Gift to sister	4,200

If Nancy had given her brother £3,000 in August 2020, she would have been limited to gifting the same amount to her sister in 2021/22.

Tax Saver

Using your annual exemption can save £3,000 of Inheritance Tax each year – £6,000 for a couple. Over a period of 10 years, for example, this amounts to a £30,000 reduction in the tax payable on your death, increasing to £60,000 for a couple.

- Gifts to any number of persons, but only up to £250 per person in each tax year. Where the total amount given to any one individual exceeds the amount of £250 then no part of the gift comes within the exemption.
- Marriage gifts. The amount you can give away in consideration of marriage or civil partnership depends on your relationship to the bride, groom or civil partner, as follows:

	£
By either parent	5,000
By a grandparent or great grandparent	2,500
By any other person	1,000

- Regular gifts out of income that form part of your normal expenditure. You need to be able to demonstrate that:

    - taking one year with another your regular gifts came out of income; and

    - you were left with sufficient income to maintain your usual lifestyle.

Tax Saver

Glyn Fielding, who lives alone, has an annual after-tax income of around £30,000. He has a modest lifestyle. He spends about £20,000 a year on his home, food, recreation, holidays and other living expenses.

His brother, Luke, who is married, is not so fortunate. Glyn could make regular gifts to his brother out of his annual surplus income of £10,000, free of Inheritance Tax.

Over 10 years Glyn might save £40,000 in Inheritance Tax.

- Lifetime gifts and bequests on death to charities and 'qualifying' political parties, without limit.

Your home

These days many of us feel an increasing need during our lifetime to help our children:

- meet the costs of university or other further education; and

- later on in life, towards a deposit on a home.

Perhaps you can only look to your home, where the greatest part of your wealth is tied up, as a source of funds to help your children? But how and what you do with your home has ramifications for Inheritance Tax. If:

- you gift your home and move out you can come back to visit or make short stays without incurring an Inheritance Tax charge;

- you give your home away but continue to live there you must pay the new owner a commercial rent in order to avoid Inheritance Tax;

- you sell your home, then whatever amount from the sale proceeds you give to your children will be outside of Inheritance Tax provided you survive for seven years from the date of the gift (but if you then move in with them you will be exposed to an Income Tax charge on a 'pre-owned asset'); or

- you give your home to your children and they move in with you, you will not have avoided Inheritance Tax as this will count as a 'gift with reservation of benefit'.

For couples, how you own your home determines the way in which it is passed on when you die, as follows:

Ownership	Beneficiary
Joint tenancy between spouses or civil partners	The survivor, automatically
Tenancy in common	In accordance with the will of the deceased, his or her share can be divided between the surviving spouse, partner and their children

Business property

Transfers in lifetime or on death, subject to certain conditions, of eligible business assets and interests in businesses qualify for relief from Inheritance Tax. There are two rates:

- 100 per cent for:
  - unincorporated businesses;
  - all holdings of unquoted shares in qualifying companies;
  - unquoted shares, including those traded on the AIM market.
- 50 per cent for:
  - shares giving control of a quoted company;
  - land, buildings, machinery or plant used in a partnership or controlled company where the transferor is a partner or controlling shareholder.

Agricultural property

The reliefs applying to agricultural land and buildings are similar to those for business property. Subject to certain minimum ownership and use conditions, the two rates are again:

- 100 per cent for:
  - land and buildings where the transferor has vacant possession, or the right to obtain it, within 12 months;
  - agricultural property let for periods exceeding 12 months where letting commenced on or after 1 September 1995.
- 50 per cent for:
  - other qualifying property.

Rates of tax payable

On your death Inheritance Tax is payable on:

- the net value of your estate immediately before your demise; and
- any PET or CLT made in the previous seven years.

The amount of Inheritance Tax payable is determined by the following table:

Cumulative chargeable transfers (£)	Rate (%)
0–325,000	0
Over 325,000	40*

*A reduced rate of 36 per cent is charged where at least 10 per cent of the net estate after taking off:
- all reliefs and expenditure; and
- the available nil rate band,
is left to charity.

The tax due on each chargeable gift or the value of your estate on death is dependent upon the cumulative value of all other chargeable transfers in the previous seven years.

Taper relief

A method of tapering relief applies where a donor dies within seven years of making a gift. It is not the gift, but the amount of tax, that is reduced. The Inheritance Tax is worked out at the rate prevailing as at the date of death and then reduced in accordance with the following table:

Number of years between gift and death	Percentage of IHT payable
Not more than 3	100
Between 3 and 4	80
Between 4 and 5	60
Between 5 and 6	40
Between 6 and 7	20

Gavin Wood, a bachelor, made his nephew, Rhys, a cash gift of £350,000 on 4 May 2016. Gavin died in November 2021 leaving an estate of £400,000.

As Gavin did not survive for seven years, Rhys has to pay tax of £3,040 on his gift, calculated as follows:

	£
Cash gift	350,000
Less: Gavin's annual exemption limits for 2014/15 and 2015/16	6,000
	344,000
Less: Nil rate band at the date of Gavin's death	325,000
Tax payable on	19,000
Inheritance Tax thereon @ 40 per cent	7,600
Less: Taper Relief (60 per cent for surviving five years)	4,560
Tax payable	3,040

It follows that there is no benefit of tapering relief where a PET, or the cumulative total of a number of PETs combined with any chargeable lifetime transfers, is within the limit of the nil rate band as at the date of death.

Family home allowance

A family home allowance, which will eventually be worth £175,000, is added to the existing £325,000 nil rate band.

This allowance started at £100,000 for deaths in 2017/18 and rises in increments of £25,000 each tax year to a maximum of £175,000 in 2020/21.

It will then increase in line with the Consumer Prices Index (CPI) from 2021 to 2022 onwards.

Known as the Residence Nil Rate Band (RNRB) it applies to the estate of an individual who:

- dies after 5 April 2017;
- owns a home, or a share in one, which is part of their estate;
- has a net estate not exceeding £2 million; and
- leaves the home, or a share of it, to their direct descendants.

A direct descendant of an individual is:

- a child, grandchild or other lineal descendant; or
- a wife, husband or civil partner of a lineal descendant (incorporating their widower, widow or surviving civil partner).

For the purpose of this allowance a child is one who:

- has been their stepchild at any time;
- has been adopted;
- was fostered by them during their lifetime; or
- was under 18 when they were made a guardian or special guardian.

Other features of this new allowance are:

- if any part of the allowance is not used it can be transferred to the estate of the surviving spouse or partner. This rule still applies even if the first death was before 6 April 2017;
- for net estates worth more than £2 million, the allowance reduces by £1 for every £2 over this amount;
- it does not apply to lifetime gifts;
- it only applies to one home which the deceased must have lived in at some time; and
- for house moves after 7 July 2015, and subject to certain conditions, it remains available to anyone who downsizes or ceases to own a home.

Roy Fisher died on 19 July 2022. In his Will he left a home valued at £220,000 and other assets worth £110,000 to his three children. He was survived by his wife, Angela, who inherited the remainder of his estate.

	£	£
Value of Roy's estate		330,000
Less:		
Residence nil rate band	100,000	
Basic nil rate band (part)	230,000	330,000
Taxable estate		Nil

The full amount of the residence nil rate band at the date of John's death has been fully utilized. The balance of the basic nil rate band of £120,000 is available to work out the Inheritance Tax payable on Angela's death.

Transferable nil rate band

Any part of the nil rate band not used on the first death of a married couple or civil partners is not lost. It is available to all survivors of a marriage or civil partnership.

It does not matter when the first spouse of a marriage died; it can have occurred at any time. However, for civil partnerships, the first death must be later than 4 December 2005 when the Civil Partnership Act came into effect.

Any amount of the unused nil rate band can only be transferred from one spouse to the surviving spouse when their relationship is ended by the death of one of them. In cases of divorce where one party to the broken marriage subsequently dies, the relief will not be available.

On the death of the survivor:

- the percentage limit of the nil rate band applying on the death of the first spouse or civil partner that was unused is applied to the nil rate band when the survivor dies; and

- the resulting amount is added to the survivor's own nil rate band.

Melvin Churchill died on 4 January 2010, leaving his estate of £200,000 to his wife, Eileen. She passed away on 10 December 2019, with an estate worth £600,000 divided between their four children.

When Melvin died, no part of the nil rate band at the time of £312,000 was used. Therefore, the nil rate band on Eileen's death is doubled to £650,000 and there is no Inheritance Tax to pay on her death.

Janice Timms died on 21 July 1996. Her estate amounted to £400,000. In her will she left legacies of £60,000 to each of her two children and the balance of her wealth to her husband, Colin. He passed away on 9 February 2019, having spent his last five years in a nursing home. His estate was worth £620,000 spread equally between the two children.

When Janice died the nil rate band was £200,000, of which 60 per cent (£120,000) was used against the legacies to her two children, leaving 40 per cent to transfer to Colin on his death earlier this year. Colin's nil rate band of £325,000 is increased by 40 per cent to £455,000, leaving Inheritance Tax at 40 per cent payable on £165,000.

Someone who has lost more than one spouse or civil partner can bring forward all or part of any unused nil rate band on the estates of more than one of them. However, the total percentage of these unused nil rate bands is restricted to a maximum of 100 per cent between them.

Marcia Bell died at home on 3 October 2019 leaving an estate valued at £850,000. She had been married twice. Her first husband, Howard, passed away on 22 May 1991 with an estate worth £180,000, of which £42,000 was inherited by their children with the balance to Marcia. At that time the nil rate band was £140,000, so Howard's estate used 30 per cent leaving 70 per cent for Marcia.

Just over three years later Marcia married Vernon. He died on 19 August 2007 leaving one half of his £240,000 estate to the children by his first marriage, and £120,000 to Marcia. By August 2007 the tax-free allowance had gone up to £300,000, so Vernon's estate accounted for 40 per cent with 60 per cent left for Marcia.

In working out the Inheritance Tax payable on Marcia's estate, which she left to the children of her marriage to Howard, her executors can take into account the unused percentages of 70 per cent and 60 per cent, totalling 130 per cent, brought forward from both Howard's and Vernon's deaths. However, she can only inherit a maximum of 100 per cent, giving a nil rate band of £650,000 on her death and with Inheritance Tax payable of £20,000 calculated as follows:

	£	£
Value of Marcia's estate		850,000
Less:		
Total of basic nil rate bands	650,000	
Residence nil rate band	150,000	800,000
Tax payable on		50,000
Inheritance Tax @ 40 per cent		20,000

Death

When someone dies, their assets pass into their estate to be administered by their personal representatives. Their main duties and responsibilities are to:

- gather in the assets of the deceased;
- settle their debts;
- pay out any legacies; and then
- distribute their remaining assets to the residuary beneficiaries.

It may also be necessary to complete a full Inheritance Tax Return and submit the form together with an application for a grant of:

- probate where there is a Will; or
- administration where there is no Will.

The Return must:

- be lodged within 12 months of the date of death; and
- include information about previous transfers and gifts in order that the amount of Inheritance Tax payable can be calculated.

In order to help your executors when the time comes, you are well advised to:

- let them know where your Will is kept;
- maintain up-to-date details of all your assets and where the supporting certificates and documents are stored; and
- keep complete records of your lifetime gifts.

Conrad Huxtable, a widower, died on 14 May 2021, leaving his entire estate to his son. He did not make any gifts in the seven years leading up to his death. His assets and unpaid bills at the time were:

	Value	
Assets	**£**	**£**
Home	460,000	
Household effects	4,000	
Car	3,000	
Building society account	20,000	
National Savings	8,000	
Individual Savings Accounts	13,000	
Bank current account	1,500	
Outstanding State Pension	540	
Cash	60	
		510,100
Less:		
Allowable deductions		
Funeral expenses	1,410	
Income tax	620	
Household bills	440	
Car repair	230	
		2,700
Net value of estate		507,400
Less:		
Residence nil rate band	150,000	
Basic nil rate band	325,000	475,000
Tax payable on		32,400
Inheritance Tax @ 40 per cent		12,960

* When Conrad's wife died her entire nil rate band was used in working out the tax on her estate.

The tax is payable out of Conrad Huxtable's estate by the executors of his Will.

Joshua Winterbottom, a bachelor, who had lived in a nursing home for many years, died on 9 January 2021. He left an estate worth £620,000. Under his Will, Joshua bequeathed legacies totalling £40,000 to a number of charities with the balance of his estate to his nieces and nephews.

The Inheritance Tax payable by his executors is £91,800 as follows:

	£	£
Value of estate		620,000
Less:		
Legacies to charities	40,000	
Nil rate band	325,000	365,000
Tax payable on		255,000
Inheritance Tax @ 36 per cent		91,800

The rate of Inheritance Tax is 36 per cent as the charitable legacies of £40,000 are more than 10 per cent of Joshua's estate after taking off the nil rate band (£620,000 – £325,000 = £295,000 x 10 per cent = £29,500).

For help and advice on probate and Inheritance Tax following a death you can call HMRC on 0300 123 1072.

Sales at a loss

Relief from Inheritance Tax is due on certain assets sold within specified time limits after death for less than their values at the date of death:

- for quoted securities the period is one year; and
- in the case of land and buildings, the time limit extends to four years.

The relief is available to the 'appropriate person', namely the person who pays the tax. All sales by that person in the respective periods must be aggregated. As a result, losses can be restricted or eliminated by profits so that the relief may be reduced or even lost. When this type of relief is claimed, the sale proceeds, before selling expenses, are substituted for the valuation at death. The Inheritance Tax liability is then reworked.

Payment of tax

Primarily liable for the payment of Inheritance Tax are:

- the transferor in respect of chargeable lifetime gifts; and
- the personal representatives on death.

Personal representatives can draw on funds held in a deceased's bank and building society accounts solely for the purpose of paying any Inheritance Tax that is due before the Grant of Probate can be issued. The payment dates for Inheritance Tax are:

Type of charge	Due date for payment
Chargeable lifetime gifts	Six months after the end of the month in which the gift was made
PETs that become taxable on death, and the charge on death	Six months after the end of the month in which death itself occurred

There is an option to pay the tax due on some types of asset by 10 equal annual instalments. For lifetime transfers that are, or become, chargeable, this instalment option is only available if the tax is borne by the transferee. The first amount is, however, payable on the normal due date.

The assets concerned are:

- land and buildings;
- controlling shareholdings;
- unquoted shares, subject to certain conditions; and
- businesses.

Where the relevant asset is disposed of during the instalment paying period, all the outstanding instalments of Inheritance Tax become immediately payable.

Interest and penalties

Interest is chargeable on Inheritance Tax liabilities from the due date until the date of payment. At the time of going to print, the rate of interest is 2.75 per cent. Any repayment of tax or interest thereon carries interest presently at the much lower rate of 0.5 per cent for the period from the date it was paid until it is refunded.

Where the instalment option is in effect, no interest is charged on the outstanding instalments of Inheritance Tax, except on:

- land and buildings that do not qualify for either business or agricultural property reliefs; and
- shares and securities in investment companies.

As with your Tax Return, there are penalties for late or incorrect Returns, delays, negligence or fraud as well as the late payment of Inheritance Tax.

Excepted estates

Where no Inheritance Tax is due:

- the estate is usually referred to as an 'excepted estate'; and
- a simpler form can be submitted as part of the probate process.

The estate will generally be an excepted estate if:

- the gross value does not exceed £1 million; and
- it is classed as an exempt estate. This is where the deceased leaves everything to a spouse, civil partner or charity; or
- it is of low value; in other words under the threshold for Inheritance Tax – £325,000 for 2021/22.

But, in some cases, a full Inheritance Tax Return may still be required even if there is no tax to pay:

- depending on the assets and debts of an estate; and
- the history of lifetime giving.

Intestacy

If you die without having made a Will, your estate will be distributed under the Intestate Estate Rules. There are two tables:

- one for an unmarried individual; and
- the other for a person with a surviving spouse.

Unmarried individual	Division

Survived by:
    Children or grandchildren
    Parents
    Brothers and sisters
    Half-brothers and half-sisters
    Grandparents
    Uncles and aunts
    The Crown
	The total estate is shared in the order of priority opposite, to the exclusion of all others

Married individual with surviving spouse	Division
(1) Estate amounts to less than £250,000	All to spouse
(2) Estate exceeds £250,000 and there are children	Spouse is entitled to the personal belongings, the first £250,000 and half the remainder. The balance is shared between the children
(3) There are no children	All to spouse

The spouse must survive the intestate individual by 28 days to become entitled under the intestacy rules.

Civil partners, and the children of a civil partnership, benefit under the intestacy rules in the same way as spouses and the children of a marriage.

It follows that if:

- you have a partner; but

- are not married,

he or she will not benefit from your estate under the intestacy rules. However, they will inherit any assets, including property, which you co-own jointly.

Tax Saver

On marriage any Will you have made is revoked. You must make a new Will otherwise the intestacy rules will determine who benefits, and by how much, from your estate.

Legacies

If you are fortunate enough to receive a legacy from a member of your family or a friend, you should keep in mind the following.

- Any Inheritance Tax on a legacy will be accounted for by the executors before you receive it.
- You do not have to pay either Income Tax or Capital Gains Tax on a legacy.
- It does not need to be reported on your annual Tax Return.

How to save on Inheritance Tax

Tax Saver

Here are some hints and tips on how to minimize the impact of Inheritance Tax on both your lifetime giving and the value of your estate on death.

- First and foremost, make a Will. Otherwise your estate will devolve under the intestacy laws and maybe not in the way that you want. This is particularly relevant for co-habitees who have no entitlement where there is no Will.
- Make sure you keep your Will up to date. Your finances and the value of your estate will change over time as will your personal circumstances and those of your family.
- To make life as easy as possible for your executors, keep a file or register with up-to-date information of all your assets and where any certificates or documents are kept.
- Maintain a record of your lifetime gifts.
- Remember that gifts and transfers, during lifetime and on death, between husbands/wives and civil partners are exempt from Inheritance Tax.
- Whenever you can afford to do so, make use of the various exemptions detailed in this chapter. By giving throughout your life you will significantly cut down on the amount of Inheritance Tax payable on your estate.

- The 'normal expenditure out of income' exemption is ideal for dealing with the payment of regular premiums on life policies written in Trust for younger generations. As the policy proceeds pass to them free of tax this is, in effect, a substitute for the payment of an Inheritance Tax liability on death, which cannot otherwise be avoided.

- Non-exempt gifts or transfers should be made as early as possible to increase your chances of surviving the seven-year period. Make immediately chargeable gifts – for example transfers into settlement – before those that are potentially exempt.

- Give assets that do not qualify for relief before those that do.

- If possible give assets with low values so that they appreciate in the hands of the recipient and outside your estate.

- You could rearrange some of your investments so that you can take advantage of the generous reliefs for agricultural or business property. Companies whose shares are quoted on AIM and which are trading companies count as unquoted for business property relief purposes.

- Gifts and legacies to charities are exempt from Inheritance Tax. If you donate at least 10 per cent of your net estate to charity, the rate of Inheritance Tax payable on the balance comes down from 40 per cent to 36 per cent.

- Consider restricting the chargeable legacies for the next generations to an amount equivalent to the nil rate band for Inheritance Tax, leaving the remainder of your estate to your spouse or civil partner. He or she can then make gifts and hopefully live for a further seven years.

- In the two years after death, consider the use of a Deed of Variation in order to utilize any available exemptions that would otherwise be lost.

18
Budget measures

On 3 March 2021, Chancellor Rishi Sunak delivered his Budget Statement for the year ahead.

The measures offer continued support to individuals and businesses impacted by the Covid-19 pandemic, while also establishing how the money borrowed by the UK government during the crisis will be repaid in the years ahead.

While some changes to allowances were confirmed for the 2021/22 tax year, the Chancellor stated that several of these would be frozen in the years that follow, to help the Treasury gather larger tax receipts as the UK looks to pay down its debt.

Several notable announcements were made in the Chancellor's speech.

- An increase in the personal allowance from £12,500 in 2020/21 to £12,570 in 2021/22. However, this allowance will now be maintained at £12,570 until April 2026.

- The higher rate threshold will increase to £50,270 for the 2021/22 tax year and be maintained at this level until April 2026.

- The temporary cut in Stamp Duty Land Tax to a nil rate band of £500,000 has been extended until 30 June 2021, reducing to £250,000 on 1 July 2021, and reverting to £125,000 on 1 October 2021.

- From 2023, the universal corporation tax rate of 19 per cent will change. UK companies making profits of up to £50,000 will pay 19 per cent. Businesses making profits between £50,000 and £250,000 will pay between 19 per cent and 24 per cent through a new tiered system, while companies whose profits exceed £250,000 will pay 25 per cent.

- The tax treatment of company losses will also change. For the tax years 2021/22 and 2022/23, companies can 'carry back' losses of up to £2 million for three years, allowing them tax refunds of up to £760,000.

- A new incentive programme to encourage companies to invest in plant and machinery assets. The new 'super deduction' tax incentive allows companies to reduce their tax bill by 130 per cent of the sum invested, by investing into 'productivity-enhancing plant and machinery assets'. The scheme will initially run for two years from the 2021/22 tax year.

On 27 October 2021, Chancellor Sunak held the Autumn Budget. Held every year, this is similar to the Spring Statement, and though it focused more on industry and business, there were some announcements regarding tax. These are as follows.

- Introduction of a Health and Social Care Levy to fund social care reforms. From April 2022, this applies to employees and employers liable for Class 1 NI contributions and self-employed individuals liable for Class 4 NI contributions. Depending on their salary, employees will have to pay an additional £130 to £880 a year with employers paying an additional 1.25 per cent.

- Dividend tax to rise by 1.25 per cent from April 2022. The £2,000 dividend allowance remains frozen, and from the 2022/23 tax year basic rate dividend tax will be charged at 8.75 per cent instead of 7.5 per cent for 2021/22. Higher rate dividend taxpayers will be charged at 33.75 per cent instead of 32.5 per cent and additional rate dividend taxpayers will pay 39.35 per cent instead of 38.1 per cent respectively.

- National Living Wage set to rise on 1 April 2022 by 6.66 per cent to £9.50 an hour.

- Annual investment allowance extended to 31 March 2023, allowing for 'super deductions' to be made on qualifying plant and machinery.

Below is a summary of the proposed measures that will not take effect until 6 April 2022 or later.

2021/22 Personal Allowances

	£
Personal all individuals	12,570*

Married couples
    born before 6 April 1935
    minimum amount
	9,075**/***
	3,450***

Transferable marriage allowance	1,250****

(continued)

(Continued)

	£
Income limits	
for personal allowance	100,000
for married couple's allowance	30,200
Relief for blind person (each)	2,450

* The personal allowance reduces at the rate of £1 for every £2 of income in excess of £100,000. The personal allowance will remain at £12,570 until 2026.

** The married couple's allowance comes down by £1 for every £2 of income above the income limit of £30,200.

*** Indicates allowances where tax relief is restricted to 10 per cent.

**** Available to spouses/civil partners born after 5 April 1935.

Tax rates and bands for 2021/22

Band of taxable income (£)	Rate of tax (%)	Tax on band (£)	Cumulative tax (£)
0–37,700	20	7,540	7,540
37,701–150,000	40	44,920	52,460
Over 150,000	45		

Scottish tax rates and bands for 2021/22

Band of taxable income (£)	Rate of tax (%)	Tax on band (£)	Cumulative tax (£)
0–2,097	19	398.43	398.43
2,098 to 12,726	20	2,125.80	2,524.23
12,727 to 31,092	21	3,856.86	5,982.66
31,093–150,000	41	48,752.28	52,609.14
Over 150,000	46		

Welsh tax rates for 2021/22

From 6 April 2019 the Welsh Government has been able to:

- set its own basic, higher and additional rates of Income Tax for taxpayers living in Wales; and
- proposed that for 2021/22 the rates will be exactly the same as those paid by taxpayers resident in England and Northern Ireland.

However, unlike the Scottish Parliament, the powers devolved to the Welsh Government do not extend to setting the bands of income taxable at the three different rates.

Rates of National Insurance Contributions for 2021/22

Class 1 Contributions for employees	
National Insurance can only be deducted on earnings above the lower earnings limit	
Lower earnings limit	£120 per week
	£520 per month
	£6,240 per year
Primary threshold	£184 per week
	£797 per month
	£9,568 per year
Secondary threshold	£170 per week
	£737 per month
	£8,840 per year
Upper secondary threshold (under 21)	£967 per week
	£4,189 per month
	£50,270 per year
Apprentice upper secondary threshold (apprentices under 25)	£967 per week
	£4,189 per month

(continued)

(Continued)

Upper earnings limit	£50,270 per year
	£967 per week
	£4,189 per month
	£50,270 per year
Class 2 Contributions	
No change from 2020/21	
Class 3 Contributions	
Voluntary contributions	£15.40 per week
Class 4 Contributions for the self-employed	
Lower Profits Limit	£9,568 per year
Upper Profits Limit	£50,270 per year

From April 2022, employers and employees alike (depending on salaries) will have to pay a Health and Social Care Levy. More details on page 115.

Rates of Child Tax Credits and Working Tax Credits for 2021/22

	£
Child Tax Credit	
Family element	545
Child element (each child)	2,830
Disabled child element	3,415
Severe disability element	1,385
Working Tax Credit	
Basic entitlement	1,995
Additional couples and lone parent element	2,045
30-hour element	825
Disability element	3,220
Severe disability element	1,390
Childcare element	
Maximum eligible cost for two or more children	£300 per week
Maximum eligible cost for one child	£175 per week
Percentage of eligible cost covered	70%

Tax credits continue to taper away at a rate of 41 per cent for each £1 of family income over the first income threshold of £6,530 (£16,385 when no Working Tax Credit is claimed). The government is making a one-off payment of £500 to eligible Working Tax Credit claimants across the UK for six months until September 2021.

Pension Lifetime Allowance

The Pensions Lifetime Allowance is to be frozen at £1,073,100 in the coming years, up to and including the financial year 2025/26.

Personal Savings Allowance

For 2021/22 the tax-free Personal Savings Allowance is unchanged as follows:

Type of taxpayer	Amount of tax-free savings income (£)
Basic rate	1,000
Higher rate	500

Savings income

A zero rate still applies to the first £5,000 of taxable savings income in 2021/22. But this zero rate is only available on any part of your taxable savings income:

- of up to £5,000; and
- after taking off your personal allowance.

Tax Saver

Taking into account the Personal Savings Allowance, you will not pay tax in 2021/22 on any savings income if your taxable income from all sources does not exceed £18,570.

Dividend income

For 2021/22:

- the tax-free dividend income allowance stays at £2,000; and
- the rates of tax payable on dividends above the nil rate threshold remain as follows:

For dividends otherwise taxable at	Rate (%)
Basic rate	7.5
Higher rate	32.5
Additional rate	38.1

Note that all rates will increase by 1.25 per cent from April 2022.

Tax-free savings accounts

For 2021/22 the maximum annual amount that can be invested:

- by all qualifying individuals in an ISA remains at £20,000 of which £4,000 can be contributed into a Lifetime ISA; and
- in a Junior ISA or Child Trust Fund remains at £9,000.

Value Added Tax

The taxable turnover of a business necessitating registration for Value Added Tax remains at £85,000. The cancellation of registration limit stays at £83,000. These limits remain fixed until 31 March 2022.

Capital Gains Tax

The 2021/22 Capital Gains Tax exemption limit will remain at £12,300 up to and including 2025/26. Also remaining unchanged from 6 April 2020:

- The lifetime limit on entrepreneurs' relief in Capital Gains Tax, which was reduced from £10 million to £1 million.

- Changes made in April 2020 that affect landlords of private residences:
  - Tax relief will continue to be cut for landlords who sell a property that was once their main home.
  - The period of Principal Private Residence Relief will remain at 9 months. Individuals moving into a care home will be unaffected by this.
  - The relief from Capital Gains Tax when you let your home will still only be available when you are in shared occupancy with your tenant.
  - As revealed in the Autumn Budget 2021, the deadline for submitting a CGT return and paying tax for landlords has been extended from 30 days to 60, from the date of the completion of the sale.

Inheritance Tax

For 2021/22:

- the nil rate band is unchanged at £325,000; and
- the family home allowance remains unchanged at £175,000.

Looking into the future

Notable measures due to take effect from 6 April 2022 are as follows.

Income Tax – Personal Allowances

The Personal Allowance and higher rate threshold will be maintained at the April 2021 level until April 2026.

Value Added Tax

The VAT registration and deregistration thresholds will not change until 1 April 2024 at the earliest.

Tax Penalties

The government is reforming the penalty regime for late VAT and Income Tax payments. Under the new rules, late filings and late payments will be judged on a points-based system.

The new late payment regime will introduce penalties in line with the amount of tax owed and how late the tax due is. The government has outlined plans to introduce a new approach to interest charges and repayment interest to align VAT with other tax regimes.

The implementation dates for these changes vary. In the 2021 Budget, Rishi Sunak stated that the reforms would come into effect as follows.

- For VAT taxpayers – All periods starting on or after 1 April 2022.
- For taxpayers in Income Tax Self-Assessment (ITSA) with income over £10,000 per year – Accounting periods starting on or after 6 April 2023.
- For all other taxpayers in ITSA – Accounting periods starting on or after 6 April 2024.

Air Passenger Duty

Air Passenger Duty rates will increase in line with the Retail Price Index (RPI) from April 2022.

Updates from the Spring 2022 Statement

On 23 March 2022, Chancellor Rishi Sunak delivered his Spring Statement. His speech was primarily aimed at helping households combat day-to-day cost of living pressures, but there were some announcements that will impact people from a tax perspective.

National Insurance

The threshold at which workers will start making Class 1 and Class 4 National Insurance contributions will increase to £12,570 from July 2022. The threshold has increased by £3,000 and will save lower income earners up to £330 per year.

From 6 April, a 1.25 per cent rise in National Insurance contributions will be implemented despite repeated calls to delay the tax hike since it was announced in the Autumn Budget.

VAT

Homeowners investing in energy-saving materials such as solar panels, heat pumps or insulation will pay 0 per cent VAT for the next five years. Previously, VAT had been charged at 5 per cent.

Income Tax

From 2024, the basic-rate Income Tax is due to be cut from 20 per cent to 19 per cent. It is estimated that more than 30 million people will benefit from a tax cut of around £175 and it will be the first time the basic rate of income tax has been cut for 16 years.

Business investment

To address a lack of capital investment in UK businesses, the government has announced the Autumn Budget will see changes to research and development tax credit and cuts to tax rates on business investment.

Employment allowance for small businesses will be increased from £4,000 to £5,000.

APPENDICES

1. Flat-rate allowances for special clothing and the upkeep of tools for 2021/22

(1) Fixed rate for all occupations	£
Agricultural	100
Clothing	60
Forestry	100
Quarrying	100
Brass and copper	120
Precious metals	100
Food	60
Glass	80
Railways (non-craftspeople)	100
Uniformed prison officers	80
Uniformed bank and building society employees	60
Uniformed police officers up to and including Chief Inspector	140
Uniformed fire fighters and fire officers	80

(2) Variable rate depending on category of occupation	£
Aircrew	See Note (2)
Forces Personnel	See Note (3)
Seamen	140/165
Iron mining	100/120
Iron and steel	60/80/140

(*continued*)

(Continued)

(2) Variable rate depending on category of occupation	£
Aluminium	60/80/120/140
Engineering	60/80/120/140
Shipyards	60/80/100/140
Vehicles	60/80/140
Particular engineering	60/80/120/140
Constructional engineering	60/80/100/140
Electrical and electricity supply	60/120
Textiles and textile printing	80/120
Leather	60/80
Printing	60/100/140
Building materials	60/80/120
Wood and furniture	60/100/120/140
Building	60/80/120/140
Heating	100/120
Public service	60/80
Healthcare	80/125/185

Notes

(1) The allowances are only available to manual workers who have to bear the cost of upkeep of tools and special clothing. Other employees, such as office staff, cannot claim them.

(2) All uniformed commercial pilots, co-pilots and other flight deck crew working in the UK are entitled to a basic flat rate expenses allowance of £1,022. An additional allowance of £110 can be claimed to cover travelling expenses for certain specified activities. The basic flat rate expense allowance for cabin crew is £720.

(3) Forces Personnel can claim for the cost of laundering their uniform. The fixed annual allowance is £80 for the Royal Navy increasing to £100 for the RAF, Army and Royal Marines.

2. HMRC (VAT) notices and leaflets

No	Title
700	The VAT Guide
700/1	Who should register for VAT?
700/11	Cancelling Your Registration
700/12	How to Fill in and Submit Your VAT Return
700/18	Relief from VAT on Bad Debts
700/21	Keeping VAT Records
700/22	Making Tax Digital for VAT
700/41	Late Registration Penalty
700/42	Misdeclaration and Repeated Misdeclaration Penalties
700/43	Default Interest
700/45	How to Correct VAT Errors and Make Adjustments or Claims
700/50	Default Surcharge
700/58	Treatment of VAT Repayment Returns and Supplements
700/62	Self Billing
700/63	Electronic Invoicing
700/64	Motoring Expenses
700/65	Business Entertainment
706	Partial Exemption
727	Retail Schemes
731	Cash Accounting
732	Annual Accounting
733	Flat Rate Scheme for Small Businesses

3. Rates of National Insurance Contributions for 2021/22

Class 1 Contributions for employees

Contributions levied on all weekly earnings above £184 but that do not exceed £967

• Standard rate	12%

Earnings threshold

• Weekly	£184
• Monthly	£797
• Annual	£9,568

Upper earnings limit

• Weekly	£967
• Monthly	£4,189
• Annual	£50,270

Contributions levied on all weekly earnings in excess of £962	2%
Reduced rate for married women and widows with a valid election certificate on earnings below upper earnings limit	5.85%
Rates for men and women over state pensionable age	Nil

Class 2 Contributions for the self-employed

Weekly flat rate	£3.05
Small earnings exception	£6,515

Class 3 Voluntary contributions

Weekly rate	£15.40

Class 4 Contributions for the self-employed

On profits between £9,568 and £50,270	9%
On profits in excess of £50,270	2%

4. Social Security benefits

Taxable

Incapacity Benefit after the first 28 weeks (1) (2)

Employment and Support Allowance (contribution-based) (3)

Industrial Death Benefit Pensions

Jobseeker's Allowance

State Retirement Pension (1)

Carer's Allowance (1)

Statutory Adoption Pay

Statutory Maternity and Paternity Pay

Statutory Shared Parental Pay

Statutory Sick Pay

Widowed Parent's and Bereavement Allowances

Non-taxable

Incapacity Benefit for the first 28 weeks (1) (2)

Employment and Support Allowance (income-related) (3)

Income Support

Maternity Allowance

Child Benefit (4)

Child Tax Credit

Child Dependency Additions

Guardian's Allowance

Christmas Bonus for Pensioners

Industrial Injury Benefits

Disability Living Allowance

Personal Independence Payment (5)

Severe Disablement Allowance

Bereavement Payment (Lump Sum)

Universal Credit (6)

Housing Benefit

War Disablement Pensions

Social Fund Payments

Attendance Allowance

Vaccine Damage (Lump Sum)

Cold Weather and Winter Fuel Payments

Pension Credit

Working Tax Credit

Notes

(1) Child dependency additions to these benefits are not taxable.

(2) Existing claimants on 27 October 2008.

(3) Replaced Incapacity Benefit for new claimants from 27 October 2008.

(4) Except for those liable to the High Income Tax Charge.

(5) Replaced Disability Living Allowance for new claimants from 8 April 2013.

(6) Has been introduced to replace previous benefits.

5. Rates of main Social Security benefits for 2021/22

Weekly rate from April 2021 onwards	£
Taxable	
New State Pension – retired after 5 April 2016	179.60
Old State Pension – retired before 6 April 2016	
Single person	137.60
Married couples: both contributors – each	137.60
Wife not contributor – addition	82.45
Over 80s age addition (Old State Pension)	0.25
Bereavement support	
Higher rate – 1st payment	3,500
Higher rate – Monthly payment	350
Lower rate – 1st payment	2,500
Lower rate – Monthly payment	100
Employment and Support allowance	
Age under 25	59.20
Age 25 or over	74.70
Jobseeker's allowance	
Age under 25	59.20
Age 25 or over	74.70

(continued)

(Continued)

Couple both 18 or over	117.40
Incapacity benefit	
Long-term	114.70
Increase for age:	
• higher rate	12.15
• lower rate	6.75
Short-term (under pension age):	51.90
Short-term (over pension age):	64.10
Statutory sick pay	
Standard rate (weekly earnings threshold £120)	96.35
Statutory maternity, paternity and adoption pay	
Rate (weekly earnings threshold £120)	151.97
Non-taxable	
Personal Independence Payment	
Daily living component	
• enhanced rate	89.60
• standard rate	60.00
Mobility component	
• enhanced rate	62.55
• standard rate	23.70
Maternity allowance	
Standard rate	151.97
Child benefit	
Only or eldest child (couple or lone parent)	21.15
Each other child	14.00

(continued)

(Continued)

Weekly rate from April 2021 onwards	£
Attendance allowance	
Higher rate	89.60
Lower rate	60.00
Universal Credit*	
Single under 25	344.00
Single 25 or over	411.51
Joint claimant both under 25	490.60
Joint claimant either 25 or over	596.58

*Monthly rates.

6. HMRC (Revenue) explanatory booklets, leaflets and helpsheets

Booklets and leaflets

No	Title
IR 115	Paying for Childcare: Getting help from your employer
480	Expenses and Benefits: A tax guide
490	Employee Travel – A Tax and NIC's Guide
SE 1	Setting Up in Business
SE 2	Giving your business the best start with tax
RK BK 1	Keeping Records for Your Tax Return
HMRC 1	HMRC Decisions: What to do if you disagree
RDR 1	Residence, domicile and the remittance basis
WTC 2	Child Tax Credit and Working Tax Credit: A guide
WTC 5	Working Tax Credit – help with the costs of childcare
WTC5/CP	Working Tax Credit – Childcare element
WTC 7	Tax Credit Penalties

Helpsheets

General

HS204	Limit on Income Tax reliefs
HS223	Rent-a-Room scheme
HS253	Furnished holiday lettings
HS305	Employment-related shares and securities
HS320	Gains on UK Life Assurance policies
HS325	Other Taxable Income
HS341	Enterprise Investment Scheme: Income Tax relief
HS342	Charitable Giving
H343	Accrued Income Scheme

Employment

HS201	Vouchers, Credit Cards and Tokens
HS202	Living Accommodation
HS203	Car Benefits and Car Fuel Benefits
HS207	Non-Taxable Payments or Benefits for Employees
HS208	Payslips and Coding Notices
HS210	Assets Provided for Private Use
HS211	Employment: Residence and domicile issues

Self-employment

HS220	More than One Business
HS222	How to Calculate Your Taxable Profits
HS227	Losses
HS229	Information from Your Accounts
HS252	Capital Allowances and Balancing Charges

7. Main dates of the Self Assessment calendar: Tuesday 6 April 2021 to Tuesday 5 April 2022

Date	What happens	Who is affected
6 April 2021	2020/21 Tax Returns sent out by HMRC.	Taxpayers who need to fill in an annual Tax Return.
1 May 2021	Daily penalty of £10, up to a maximum of £900.	Taxpayers who have failed to complete their 2019/20 Tax Return.
31 July 2021	Second payment on account due for 2020/21.	Those taxpayers who make regular half-yearly payments on account.
1 August 2021	First tax geared penalty levied for failing to submit a 2019/20 Tax Return before this date.	Taxpayers who have not yet completed and sent back their 2019/20 Tax Returns.
3 August 2021	Further 5 per cent late payment penalty on tax still outstanding for 2020/21.	Late payers of tax still due for 2019/20.
31 October 2021	Filing deadline for completing and returning 2020/21 paper Tax Returns.	Taxpayers who want HMRC to: calculate their tax for 2020/21; and collect tax owing for 2020/21 of less than £3,000 through their code number in 2022/23.
31 December 2021	Non-mandatory filing deadline for 2020/21 online Tax Returns.	Online filers who want HMRC to collect tax owing for 2020/21 of less than £3,000 through their code number in 2022/23.
31 January 2022	Filing deadline for 2020/21 online Tax Returns. Payment date for the balance of tax due for 2019/20 and the first payment on account for 2020/21.	Taxpayers sent a 2020/21 Tax Return. Taxpayers who need to settle either of these liabilities.
1 February 2022	First penalty notices issued for the late filing of a 2020/21 Tax Return.	Taxpayers who were sent a 2020/21 Tax Return.
3 March 2022	First 5 per cent late payment penalty imposed for failing to pay tax due by 31 January 2022 and still outstanding on 3 March 2022.	Late payers of tax for 2020/21.

INDEX